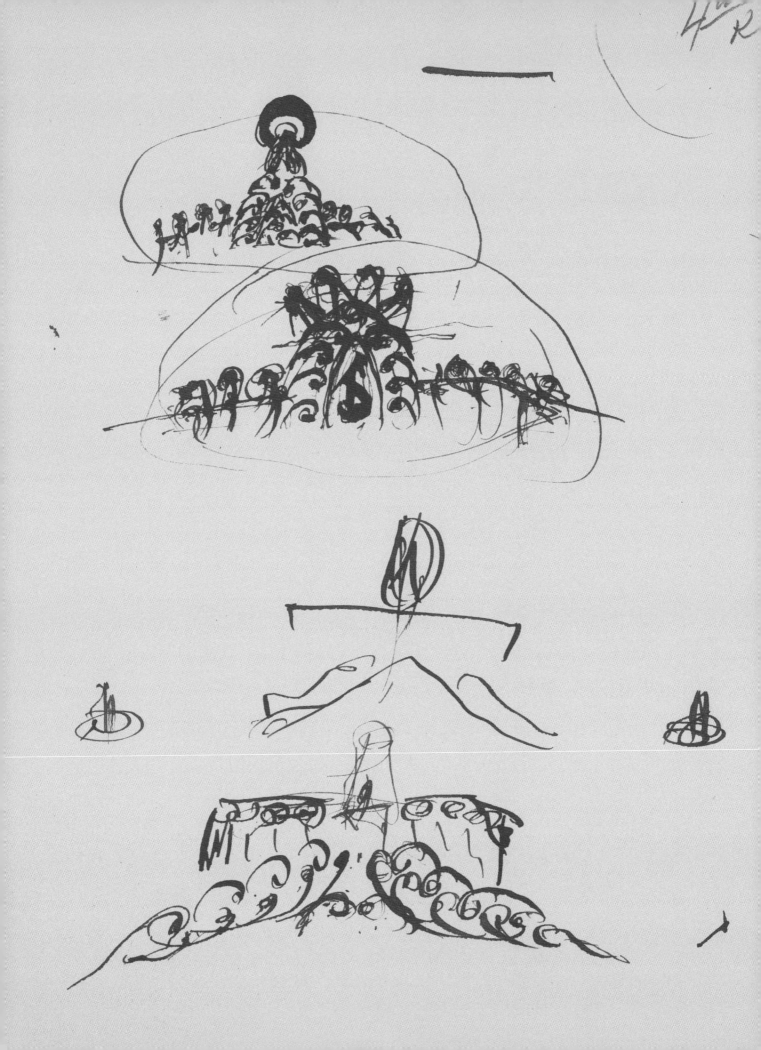

Crafting the Ballets Russes

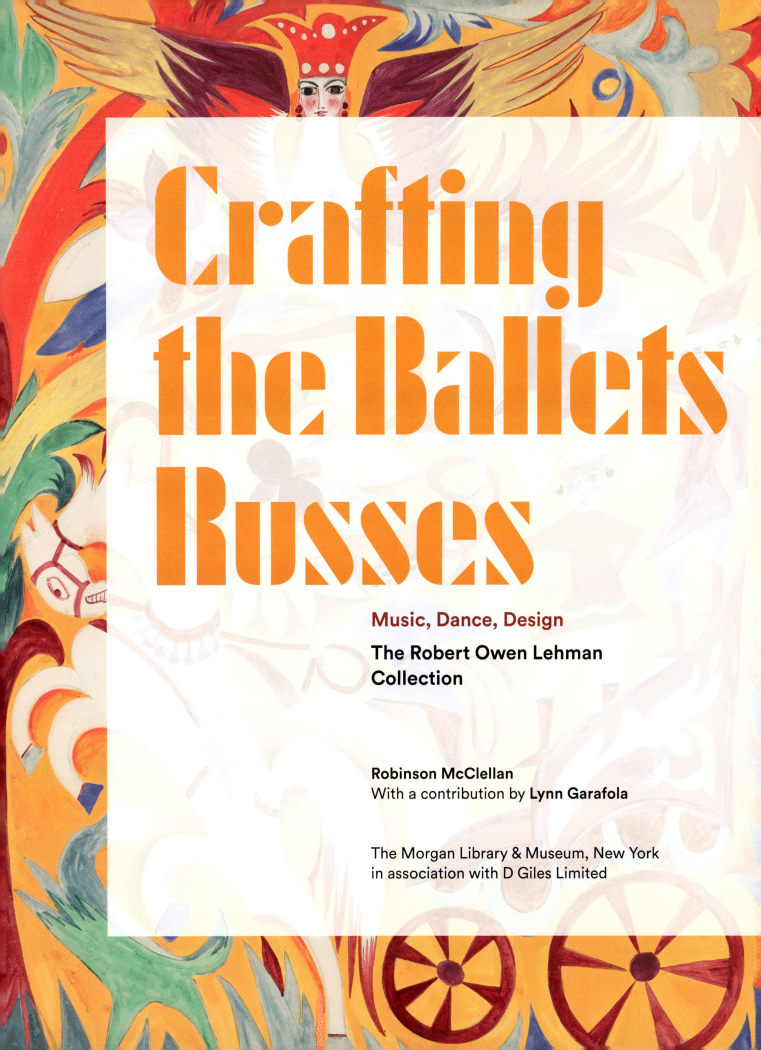

Crafting the Ballets Russes

Music, Dance, Design

The Robert Owen Lehman Collection

Robinson McClellan
With a contribution by **Lynn Garafola**

The Morgan Library & Museum, New York
in association with D Giles Limited

Published to accompany the exhibition *Crafting the Ballets Russes: The Robert Owen Lehman Collection* at the Morgan Library & Museum, New York, 28 June–22 September 2024

This exhibition is supported by the William Randolph Hearst Fund for Scholarly Research and Exhibitions, the Robert Lehman Foundation, Mr. and Mrs. Clement C. Moore II, Elizabeth and Jean-Marie Eveillard, Cynthia Hazen Polsky and Leon Polsky, and the Franklin Jasper Walls Lecture Fund. Assistance is provided by the Gladys Krieble Delmas Foundation and Hubert and Mireille Goldschmidt.

The
Morgan
Library &
Museum
100

The Morgan Library & Museum
225 Madison Avenue
New York, NY 10016
themorgan.org

GILES
An imprint of D Giles Limited
66 High Street
Lewes, BN7 1XG, UK
gilesltd.com

ISBN 978-1-913875-67-1

Library of Congress
Cataloging-in-Publication Data

Names: McClellan, Robinson, 1976– author. | Garafola, Lynn, author. | Pierpont Morgan Library.
Title: Crafting the Ballets russes : music, dance, design : the Robert Owen Lehman collection / Robinson McClellan, with a contribution by Lynn Garafola.
Description: New York : The Morgan Library & Museum, 2024. | Includes bibliographical references and index.
Identifiers: LCCN 2023051785 | ISBN 9781913875671 (hardcover)
Subjects: LCSH: Ballets russes—Exhibitions. | Ballets—20th century—Exhibitions. | Ballets—Production and direction—History—20th century. | Ballet companies—France—Paris—History—20th century. | Diaghilev, Serge, 1872–1929. | Pierpont Morgan Library—Exhibitions.
Classification: LCC ML28.P2 B2569 2024 | DDC 781.5/560944361—dc23/eng/20231128
LC record available at https://lccn.loc.gov/2023051785

For the Morgan Library & Museum
Publications Manager: Karen Banks
Editor: Ryan Newbanks
Assistant Editor: Yuri Chong
Director of Imaging & Rights: Marilyn Palmeri
Manager of Imaging & Rights: Eva Soos

For D Giles Limited
Copyedited and proofread by Sarah Kane
Produced by GILES, an imprint of D Giles Limited
Printed and bound in Europe

Designed by Barbara Glauber / Heavy Meta
Typeset in Circular, Crisol, and Martina Plantijn

Front cover: Vaslav Nijinsky and Bronislava Nijinska in *L'Après-midi d'un Faune*, Paris, May 1912. Photograph by Waléry (colorized detail; p. 69, fig. 26).

Back cover: Igor Stravinsky, "Adagio / Supplication of the Firebird" from *Firebird*, autograph manuscript, piano, extensive revisions, p. 11, [1910], inscribed 1918 (colorized detail; p. 48, fig. 11).

Front endpapers: Maurice Ravel, *La Valse*, autograph manuscript, piano, pp. 14–15, 1920 (colorized detail; p. 112, fig. 55).

Front endpapers overleaf: Bronislava Nijinska, Choreographic drawings for *Les Noces*, ca. 1923 (colorized detail; p. 94, bottom).

Pages 2–3: Natalia Goncharova, Curtain design for *Les Noces*, 1915 (detail; pp. 88–89, fig. 41).

Contents

DIRECTOR'S FOREWORD

One of several major initiatives marking the hundredth anniversary of J. P. (Jack) Morgan Jr.'s generous gift of his father's library and collection to the public, in 1924, this book and the exhibition it accompanies celebrate one of the Morgan's most cherished and widely studied holdings. The Robert Owen Lehman Collection, held on deposit at the Morgan, is considered the world's finest private gathering of music manuscripts. Amid Lehman's panoramic record of the Western music tradition, spanning Bach and Mozart to Mahler and Messiaen, lies his rich collection of French and Russian ballet manuscripts of the early twentieth century, including *Firebird*, *Petrouchka*, *Prélude à l'après-midi d'un faune*, *Les Noces*, *Bolero*, and many others, joining additional ballet manuscripts of the era in the Morgan's own music collections.

This collection, shown here for the first time, allows us to tell the story of these ballets anew by presenting music alongside the vivid stage designs and rarely seen choreographic notations for the same ballets. Together, these materials offer fresh insight into Serge Diaghilev's famed Ballets Russes troupe and its broader circle, the revitalization of ballet that energized Paris in the first decades of the twentieth century, and the composers, choreographers, and artists, each working at the top of their disciplines, who created these memorable stage spectacles both within and beyond Diaghilev's company.

Lynn Garafola's essay takes up a key story: the rise, thanks to Serge Diaghilev's probing musical sense and his unfailing taste and standards, of a stunning new repertoire of ballet scores, well represented in the Lehman Collection. Many of these scores became classics of twentieth-century concert music, and have inspired hundreds of stage productions in the intervening century.

At the core of this story is the creative process that brought these ballets to life. Robinson McClellan's essay addresses the narrative of the key creative figures—their collaborations, friendships, and rivalries. Examining the sketches, drafts, and working copies of composer, choreographer, and designer, he considers these three art forms as elements within a joint process and captures the ways in which these creators worked together to conceive and execute stage works of astonishing originality and ongoing influence.

The story of these ballets and their creators highlights the rise of women in leading creative roles. Bronislava Nijinska, who helped her brother Vaslav Nijinsky to formulate a new kind of dance in Claude Debussy's *L'Après-midi d'un Faune* (1912) and Igor Stravinsky's *Rite of Spring* (1913), became the Ballets Russes' only female choreographer in 1921. Her groundbreaking choreography defined Stravinsky's *Les Noces* (1923) and Maurice Ravel's *Bolero* (1928). Ida Rubinstein, whose riveting performances in *Cléopâtre* (1909) and *Schéhérazade* (1910) helped establish the Ballets Russes, came to rival Diaghilev as a patron of new music. After parting ways with him in 1910, she commissioned a new score from Debussy, *The Martyrdom of St. Sebastian* (1911), and produced other stage works through the 1910s and '20s. In 1928 Rubinstein founded a ballet company that drew an all-star team of Ballets Russes veterans. She commissioned new scores from Stravinsky and Ravel, hired Nijinska as choreographer, and worked with Alexandre Benois—Diaghilev's key collaborator during the early years of the Ballets Russes—to design and oversee her productions.

We extend our gratitude to the lenders who have enabled us to enrich our own holdings of music manuscripts, drawings, and ephemera with the stage designs, choreographic notation, letters, photographs, and other material. For their collegiality, we acknowledge the Library of Congress Music Division, the New York Public Library's Jerome Robbins Dance Division, Harvard University's Houghton Library, the Wadsworth Atheneum, the Metropolitan Museum of Art, the Museum of Modern Art, the Philadelphia Museum of Art, and the Mead Art Museum, as well as the private collectors who have contributed key works.

This publication and the exhibition it accompanies would not be possible without the generous support of the William Randolph Hearst Fund for Scholarly Research and Exhibitions, the Robert Lehman Foundation, Mr. and Mrs. Clement C. Moore II, Elizabeth and Jean-Marie Eveillard, Cynthia Hazen Polsky and Leon Polsky, and the Franklin Jasper Walls Lecture Fund, with assistance from the Gladys Krieble Delmas Foundation and Hubert and Mireille Goldschmidt.

Colin B. Bailey
Director, The Morgan Library & Museum

← Tamara Karsavina and Michel Fokine in *Firebird*, 1910. Reproduced in *Collection des plus beaux numéros de "Comoedia illustré" et des programmes consacrés aux ballets et galas russes depuis le début à Paris, 1909–1921*. The Morgan Library & Museum, New York, Mary Flagler Cary Music Collection.

1
Offert à Mr A. Cortot
par Mme G. Lhéry
October 1899.
Assez Lent.
p très doux
(Fl.)
Harpe
crescendo

PROLOGUE

Crafting the Ballets Russes: Music, Dance, Design— The Robert Owen Lehman Collection celebrates the Morgan Library's centennial as a public institution. Simultaneously, it marks the half century since Robert Owen Lehman's extraordinary music manuscript collection arrived at the Morgan. While the legacy of the Ballets Russes has been commemorated in revival productions by contemporary dance troupes and in exhibitions of visual iconography—costumes, set designs, and the like—presented by other institutions, never before have the musical compositions that were commissioned for the Ballets Russes been featured. The Morgan Library & Museum is uniquely poised to spotlight these works, as it conserves so many of the manuscripts and scores—many of them in the Lehman Collection—that provided the fundamental impetus for the artistic extravaganzas engineered by Serge Diaghilev.

As Lynn Garafola makes clear in her essay, music was an integral part of Diaghilev's family life. He studied piano, voice, music theory, and composition as a youth, and this rich background surely informed his discriminating musical taste and judgment. During his twenties, Diaghilev was inspired by the work of Richard Wagner, whose philosophical ideal of creating a Gesamtkunstwerk ("complete artwork")—involving a synthesis of the arts—would have a profound impact on his own aesthetic development. However, after his early compositional forays were rebuffed by the venerated composer and teacher Nikolai Rimsky-Korsakov, Diaghilev shifted his attention to the visual arts. He curated an exhibition of Russian portraits in 1905, and soon thereafter hatched a plan to introduce Russian art and music to the cosmopolitan city of Paris, culminating in the launch of Modest Mussorgsky's monumental opera *Boris Godunov* at the Paris Opéra in 1908. The following year, expanding on his early exposure to ballet at the Maryinsky Theater in St. Petersburg, Diaghilev brought Russian ballet to Paris for the first time. Drawing on his early passion and expertise in music, the visual arts, and dance, Diaghilev would weave these various art forms into a cohesive and aesthetically riveting whole that captivated audiences in Paris and beyond. He would bring together the major composers, choreographers, and costume and stage designers of the time—Nikolai Rimsky-Korsakov, Igor Stravinsky, Sergey Prokofiev, Claude Debussy, Maurice Ravel, Erik Satie, Michel Fokine, Vaslav Nijinsky, Bronislava Nijinska, Léonide Massine, Alexandre Benois, Léon Bakst, Natalia Goncharova, and Pablo Picasso, among others—to create the spectacular productions of the Ballets Russes. He grew to be an influential impresario who would animate cultural life for the next two decades, leaving a legacy that is as compelling today as it was in 1909–29. Serge Diaghilev was the right man in the right place at the right time.

As a collector of music manuscripts, so too was Robert Owen (Robin) Lehman the right man in the right place at the right time. Born into a family with a passion for fine art and collecting that undoubtedly shaped his own connoisseurship, he studied painting as a youth and throughout his college years at Yale University. But whereas Diaghilev pivoted from music to the visual arts, Lehman's interest shifted from painting to music when he moved to Paris in 1959 to study composition with the famed Nadia Boulanger. He would eventually combine his passion and expertise in music and art, becoming a documentary filmmaker. Lehman's films are known for the extraordinary way in which the music enhances the visuals, and, over a period of about a dozen years, he would win more than 150 major awards at film festivals throughout the world, including two Academy Awards and an Emmy. In his short documentary *Don't* (1974)—Lehman's first Academy Award–winning film, covering the life cycle of a monarch butterfly—the magical moment when the monarch emerges from its chrysalis is accompanied by the fluttering and lyrical strains of Chopin's *Andante spianato*. His film *Forever Young* (1980)—featuring some fascinating seniors and their wise musings on fundamental issues such as health, sex, happiness, love, and death—ends with an exuberant arrangement of Bob Dylan's iconic song. Both Diaghilev and Lehman used their artistic interests and gifts to create works that combined multiple art forms in unique ways. While Diaghilev fused music and art with dance in his stunning Ballets Russes productions, Lehman combined art, music, and videography in his original motion pictures.

The city of Paris was the catalytic epicenter for each man's growth—as an impresario, in Diaghilev's case, and as a collector, in Lehman's case. During the 1960s in Paris, while Lehman was studying with Boulanger, musical manuscripts were readily available, and for reasonable prices. Fortuitously, he had the requisite musical skills and acumen to seek out only the very best compositional specimens. Just as the impresario would draw on the expertise of multiple artists, so would the collector rely on many fellow musicians, artists, dealers, and publishers—Alfred Cortot, Doda Conrad, Igor Stravinsky, the Princesse de Polignac, Robert Legouix, Albi Rosenthal, Thierry Bodin, and Léonide Massine, among others—to assist him in acquiring his magnificent collection of music manuscripts.

As a composer himself, Robin Lehman has always been especially interested in collecting manuscripts that reveal a composer's thinking, i.e., working drafts or short scores, as opposed to clean, fair copies of complete works. He views them essentially as lessons in music composition, and curator Robinson McClellan reflects this approach in his essay and in his conception of the exhibition, *Crafting the Ballets Russes: The Robert Owen Lehman Collection*, offering a window into the creative process of the composers, choreographers, dancers, and stage designers that were encouraged, inspired, and at times cajoled by Serge Diaghilev to collaborate on a Gesamtkunstwerk that was ultimately greater than the sum of its parts. We invite you to appreciate and admire their artistic synergy in this exhibition and its accompanying catalogue.

Marie Rolf
Professor Emerita, Eastman School of Music,
University of Rochester

Diaghilev— Man of Music

Lynn Garafola

↑ **Fig. 1.** Léon Bakst (1866–1924), *Portrait of Serge Diaghilev and His Nanny*, 1906. State Russian Museum, St. Petersburg.

n the mid-1970s, when I first began my research on Serge Diaghilev's Ballets Russes, it was still possible to see many of its works in live performance. *Les Sylphides* was a staple of American Ballet Theatre, the curtain-raiser, often, for *Giselle*. The company had *Firebird*, the original Michel Fokine version, with the magnificent scenery and costumes Natalia Goncharova had designed in 1926. For the Joffrey Ballet, Christmas meant *Petrouchka*, another Fokine work, seen in its original setting by Alexandre Benois—a work that like *Les Sylphides* had long held its own in the international repertory. Later came all-Diaghilev nights, when Vaslav Nijinsky's *L'Après-midi d'un Faune* (*Afternoon of a Faun*) and Léonide Massine's *Parade*, with its Picasso designs, joined *Petrouchka* in evoking Diaghilev's multi-disciplinary magic. Balanchine may have rejected the collaborationist ethos of the Ballets Russes, but from the start his New York City Ballet danced a stripped-down *Apollon Musagète* (now renamed *Apollo*) and *Prodigal Son* with the original Rouault designs that even today elicit applause. He choreographed a new version of *Firebird* (with designs by Chagall), while the company's associate director, Jerome Robbins, remade *Afternoon of a Faun*, setting it in a ballet studio. Meanwhile, at the Four Seasons, in the passage between the restaurant's two dining rooms, Picasso's huge curtain for Massine's *Le Tricorne* hung for decades. (It is now at the New-York Historical Society; see p. 101.)

The 1980s added to the stock of living Ballets Russes performances. Bronislava Nijinska's *Les Noces* and *Les Biches*—long ignored by U.S. companies—returned to repertory, first at the Oakland Ballet, then in New York and elsewhere, opening a whole new perspective on the history of ballet neoclassicism. Nijinsky's *Rite of Spring*, as recreated by Millicent Hodson and Kenneth Archer for the Joffrey Ballet, played to sold-out houses, while Dance Theatre of Harlem's revival of Fokine's *Schéhérazade* and *Prince Igor* found large audiences. Some revivals, like Nijinska's *Le Train Bleu*, with costumes by Chanel and a front curtain by Picasso, dazzled the eye, as did the new version of *Firebird* by John Taras that Geoffrey Holder set in an African rainforest. Meanwhile, postmodern choreographers such as Lucinda Childs and Trisha Brown embarked on collaborations with contemporary visual artists that recalled Diaghilev's own with painters of an earlier generation.

By the early 2000s this revivalist impulse had run its course. Companies and budgets shrank, artists' estates dramatically increased royalties, and new artistic directors arrived. Scenery and costumes were sold to save storage fees. Performances of the historical repertory dwindled. The 2023 centenary of *Les Noces* went all but unnoticed, yet it was the single most important Diaghilev production of the 1920s.[1] Although recordings exist of some Ballets Russes works, many more were never filmed, and the footage that does exist is often silent and fragmentary. So

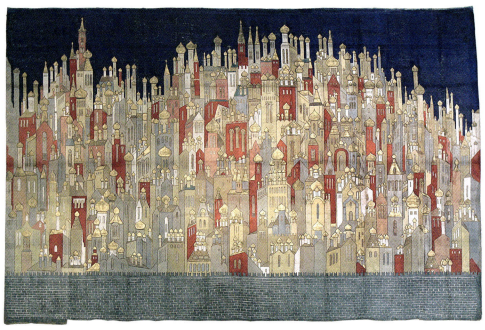

what remains of the repertory that changed the course of ballet in the early part of the twentieth century? Has it all gone?

Of course, the vast majority of dances vanish within a decade of their creation.[2] However, even as they slip into the limbo of non-performance, most ballets leave traces—images, designs, recollections—that allow us to conjure them up in the privacy of the imagination. In the case of the Diaghilev repertory, a rich cache of designs and other visual iconography survives. But an even greater cache is the music that formed the backbone of the Diaghilev enterprise. For Diaghilev, "music was the basis of the ballet," composer Vittorio Rieti once remarked, and this was true as well for his choreographers and dancemakers.[3] All had studied music, and in the case of Balanchine and Nijinska were able to handle scores of great complexity. All, moreover, choreographed to the music, exemplifying, despite their different approaches, what choreomusicologist Stephanie Jordan has called Diaghilev's "music-based modernism." Thus, it is through the company's soundscapes—the music chosen, commissioned, and transformed by Diaghilev in tandem with his choreographers—that one can not only re-experience the kinetic and rhythmic expressiveness of individual works but also appreciate a crucial part of the legacy of the Ballets Russes. Diaghilev had a "voracious appetite for all kinds of music," composer Nicolas Nabokov has written, as well as the "gift of detecting . . . the quality of a piece of music" and its originality.[4] If ballet acquired a remarkable body of new music in the early twentieth century, it was chiefly thanks to Diaghilev's knowledge, discernment, passion, and imagination. With reason, composer William Schuman later claimed, "the great patron of twentieth-century music has been the art of dance."[5] The renaissance of ballet that began in Europe on the eve of World War I was as much a musical as a choreographic phenomenon.

Born in 1872, Diaghilev grew up in the remote Russian city of Perm, in a family that wove music into the fabric of everyday life. Music-making was a gentry pastime in provincial Russia, and the Diaghilev home, with its corner ballroom where weekly concerts were given, was the city's "Athens."[6] Diaghilev sang, studied piano, wrote his first compositions, and gave his first public performance in Perm. He sight-read with ease and knew Mussorgsky's *Boris Godunov* by heart, a taste that set him apart from the young cosmopolitans he would meet in St. Petersburg.[7] Perm lay nearly a thousand miles east of Moscow. Forests stretched as far as the eye could see, past towns with onion-domed churches and estates, like Bikbarda, where the Diaghilevs spent long summers surrounded by peasants who worked the family lands. Diaghilev carried these heartland memories to the Russian capital, where they mingled with the sights and sounds of the metropole. "I never leave the theater," he wrote to his stepmother.[8] "[Adelina] Patti is still here concertizing. . . . Medea Figner is singing; they're offering a subscription to Sembrich and Cotogni;[9] and on top of that there are the first performances of *Prince Igor*. . . . Imagine what an effect all this has on a poor, country boy from Perm!"[10] And there was ballet. At the Maryinsky Theater, Diaghilev attended early performances of *The Sleeping Beauty*, a ballet his company would later revive, with its marvelous Tchaikovsky score. He discovered the repertory of Marius Petipa, who had ruled the Imperial Ballet since the 1860s—*La Bayadère*, *Don Quixote*, *Daughter of Pharaoh*, and innumerable now-forgotten works.

At the Maryinsky, he also discovered the operas of Richard Wagner. In 1892, with his cousin and first love, Dmitry Filosofov, he traveled to the master's shrine in Bayreuth where they attended the whole of the Ring cycle in addition to *Parsifal*, *Tristan und Isolde*, and *Die Meistersinger*. Diaghilev was transfixed. "The conversations about Wagner never end," he wrote to his stepmother. "I am certain that people who . . . see no point in living, . . . people who despair to the point of bringing their life to an . . . end—all of them should come here," as if Wagner's music and the very air of Bayreuth could heal the traumas of Europe's cosmopolitan elites.[11] Diaghilev himself went back again and again. Wagnerian ideas permeated his future theatrical work, from its pervasive aestheticism to its emphasis on Gesamtkunstwerk, an ideal of fusion and collaboration in the creation of an artistic whole.

Ardent Wagnerian though he may have been, in St. Petersburg Diaghilev was welcomed into music circles linked to Russia's nationalist group of composers known as the "Kuchka"—"The Five" or "Mighty Handful." "This is highly significant," Diaghilev's biographer Sjeng Scheijen observes, "because the work of the Five would come to occupy a prominent place in the repertoire of the Ballets Russes up until the

↑   **Fig. 3.** Richard Wagner, [1883]. Photograph by Rogelio de Egusquiza Barrena (1845–1915). The Morgan Library & Museum, New York, gift of Hester Diamond, 2012.

First World War."[12] Diaghilev produced three of Rimsky-Korsakov's operas (*Ivan the Terrible*, *Le Coq d'Or*, and *May Night*), and his tone poem *Schéhérazade*, one of his company's most popular ballets. Borodin was a close second, with *Prince Igor*, staged both as an opera and a stand-alone ballet adapted from the second-act Polovtsian Dances, a work that long survived in repertory. One or another of Russia's nationalist composers provided music for a half-dozen other ballets and all or part of an additional handful of operas, including Mussorgsky's *Boris Godunov* and *Khovanshchina*.[13]

Law school notwithstanding, Diaghilev was immersed in musical study. He took voice lessons, spoke about enrolling in the conservatory, and studied music theory and composition. He was also composing, producing chamber works, romances, songs, a sonata for cello and piano, a violin sonata, even scenes for an opera inspired by Pushkin's *Boris Godunov* that he performed at intimate gatherings. Few appreciated the opera fragments. Benois shrugged them off as "broad melodies" combining "elements of Mussorgsky with reminders of Tchaikovsky."[14] In 1894 Diaghilev took his work to Rimsky-Korsakov, one of Russia's leading composers and a powerful figure at the St. Petersburg conservatory. Rimsky's response was damning. Characterizing Diaghilev as a young man "who fancies himself a composer," he dismissed the compositions as "absurd" and "told him so bluntly," whereupon Diaghilev "became offended and . . . declared . . . that nevertheless he believes in himself and his gifts . . . [and] will never forget this day."[15]

That day changed the course of Diaghilev's life. Unwilling to become a third-rate composer, he gave up writing music and shifted his focus to the visual arts, quickly emerging as a fine arts curator and collector, and in 1898 founding the journal *Mir iskusstva* (World of Art). The following year he joined the staff of Prince Serge Volkonsky, a young aesthete who had recently become Minister of the Imperial Theaters. Two years later Diaghilev was dismissed, and with that dismissal went all hope of a position in the civil service. Undaunted, he embarked on his most ambitious undertaking yet, unveiling in 1905, as the Revolution of that year got underway, a stunning display of more than 2,000 portraits by 400 artists entitled "Exhibition of Historic Russian Portraits."[16] It turned out to be Diaghilev's last project in Russia. The following year he curated another splendid exhibition, this one in Paris at the Salon d'Automne, in which he revealed a history of Russian art beginning with icons and ending with the young generation of painters. At the same time he returned to music—not as a creative artist but as the curator of a "judiciously chosen" program tracing the "development of the Russian

Rimsky-Korsakow

↑ **Fig. 4.** Nikolai Rimsky-Korsakov, n.d. The Morgan Library & Museum, New York, James Fuld Collection.

school from Glinka . . . to its most modern representatives."[17] Performed in the exhibition's central gallery, the concert launched him as an impresario in the export of Russian art.

In the years that followed, Diaghilev's activities moved in an increasingly performative direction. The Russian Historical Concerts, a series he produced at the Paris Opéra in 1907, offered a grand overview of Russian music, with performances by Russia's greatest musicians. Of the composers represented at the festival, most would later figure prominently in the Ballets Russes, with several of their programmed works either adapted or incorporated into various ballets. Ironically, the "lion" of the season was none other than the sixty-three-year-old Rimsky-Korsakov, "the master, the purest and undisputed glory of Russian music," in the words of an admiring French critic. Letting bygones be bygones, Diaghilev had persuaded Rimsky to conduct several of his works in Paris.[18] Finally, in 1908, Diaghilev returned to the Opéra with his first full-fledged theatrical production, *Boris Godunov*, never before heard in the West, with the incomparable Fedor Chaliapin in the title role. The work, which Diaghilev would produce again in 1913 and 1914 for performances in Paris and London, dominated Russian émigré opera until the 1930s.

In 1909, and at least once every year until 1914, Diaghilev returned to Paris with the company of dancers that would seal his reputation as a brilliant and highly innovative producer of ballets and lead in 1911 to the formation of the troupe known as the Ballets Russes. From the first Diaghilev rejected the full-evening productions, undistinguished music, and mediocre designs of the Maryinsky's standard choreographic fare. Instead, he highlighted the repertory of one-act ballets and other short works that Fokine was beginning to develop in St. Petersburg. Music played a key role in this development. The "new ballet," Fokine declared in 1914, "does not demand 'ballet music' of the composer . . . ; it accepts music of every kind provided only that it is good and expressive."[19] Like Isadora Duncan, Fokine combed the nineteenth-century repertory, choreographing to Chopin (*Les Sylphides*) and Schumann (*Carnaval*), which raised the hackles of critics who took exception to concert music being pressed into service for ballet.

Diaghilev was equally high-handed but more nationalist-minded, enveloping the choreography in waves of Russian sound. "There was a moment," wrote a columnist after the first performance of the Polovtsian Dances in 1909, "when the entire hall . . . was ready to stand up and actually rush to arms. That vibrant music, . . . the dazzle of the multicolored costumes seemed for a moment to dizzy the Parisian audience, stunned by the fever and madness of movement."[20] *Schéhérazade*, which premiered the following year, thrilled novelist Arnold Bennett, with its "shocking brutality," frenzy, and "hard breathing of the executioners."[21]

From the outset Diaghilev curated the company's music. He hired the then little-known Igor Stravinsky to orchestrate *Les Sylphides*; expanded the score of *Cléopâtre*; dropped the chorus from the Polovtsian Dances to create a stand-alone dance work; and excised parts of Rimsky's symphonic suite to make *Schéhérazade* viable as a one-act ballet with an original libretto. And even before the 1909 season was over, he began "scouring France as well as Russia for . . . composers," according to M. D. Calvocoressi, a music critic who worked closely with Diaghilev during his first seasons in Paris.[22] It took several years before music by either Debussy or Ravel was heard on the Diaghilev stage,[23] and few of the other composers recommended by "Calvo" ever received a commission. But in 1910 Diaghilev produced the first ballet by the composer he called his "first son." With *Firebird*, the twenty-eight-year-old Stravinsky tasted international fame as the "heir apparent" of "the great Russians" that Calvocoressi and his musical colleagues "loved so well."[24]

Stravinsky was not Diaghilev's first choice for *Firebird* (three laggards had preceded him), but it was providential. By the time Diaghilev

↑   **Fig. 5.** Igor Stravinsky, around the time he met Serge Diaghilev and Michel Fokine. Fabrice Herrault Collection.
→   **Fig. 6.** Igor Stravinsky (1882–1971), *Firebird*, orchestral parts, copyist manuscript, annotated by musicians, ca. 1910–29. From the library of Serge Diaghilev. The Morgan Library & Museum, New York, Mary Flagler Cary Music Collection.

died in 1929, Stravinsky had composed many of the company's greatest works, including *Petrouchka*, *The Rite of Spring*, *Les Noces*, and *Apollon Musagète*, and stood at the forefront of the modern school. Diaghilev had "an immense flair for recognizing the potentiality of success in a piece of music," Stravinsky said many years later. "[W]hen I played him the beginning of the *Sacre* . . . he realized at once the seriousness of my new musical speech [and] its importance."[25] These works underscored not only the continued "Russianness" of Diaghilev's expatriated enterprise, but also its commitment to modernism: the arrival of the Ballets Russes in Paris coincided with the appearance of Cubism. Shedding the conventions of nineteenth-century ballet music, Diaghilev's composers created a body of music for dance that easily found a place in the concert hall.

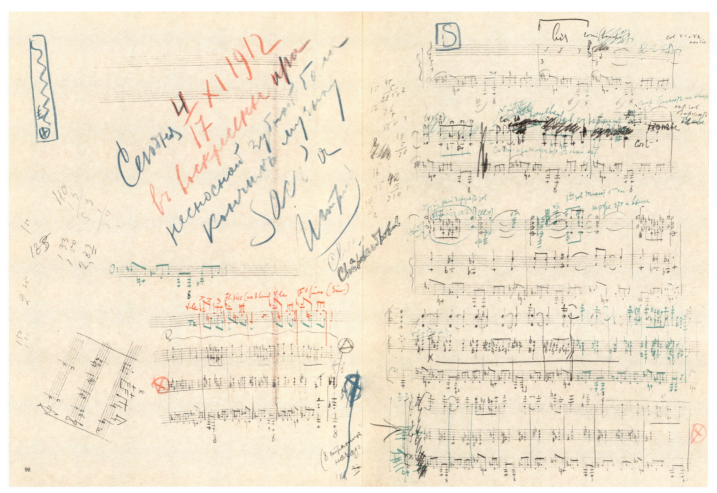

↑   **Fig. 7.** Igor Stravinsky (1882–1971), *The Rite of Spring / Le Sacre du Printemps: Sketches, 1911–1913; Facsimile Reproductions from the Autographs*, pp. 96–[97] ([London]: Boosey & Hawkes, 1969). The Morgan Library & Museum, New York, Mary Flagler Cary Music Collection. In blue and red, Stravinsky writes, "Today Sunday 4/17 XI 1912 with an unbearable toothache I finished the music of Sacre. I Strav Clarens Chatelard Hotel."

As season after season unfolded—and especially after the launch of the Ballets Russes in 1911 as a year-round company headquartered in Western Europe—the breadth of Diaghilev's musical knowledge and his increasingly adventurous musical choices were revealed. *Petrouchka*, the second of Stravinsky's "Russian" works, entered the repertory in 1911. The following year saw the first of Diaghilev's French commissions come to fruition—Ravel's *Daphnis and Chloë* and Reynaldo Hahn's *Le Dieu Bleu*.[26] Despite publishing the libretto, Debussy had abandoned *Masques et Bergamasques*. But now, with Nijinsky using his music in *L'Après-midi d'un Faune*, the composer was in the public eye, dragged into the fracas produced by the ballet's choreographic minimalism and final masturbatory gesture (see p. 71). However, Diaghilev was still intent on Debussy's composing an original ballet for the company, and Debussy, needing money, succumbed over lunch to the "terrifying but charming man" and agreed to compose *Jeux*.[27] Nijinsky had devised the scenario

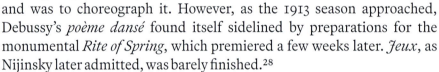

and was to choreograph it. However, as the 1913 season approached, Debussy's *poème dansé* found itself sidelined by preparations for the monumental *Rite of Spring*, which premiered a few weeks later. *Jeux*, as Nijinsky later admitted, was barely finished.[28]

Debussy was not the only French composer shabbily treated by Diaghilev. In 1911 Diaghilev announced, but then canceled, the premiere of Paul Dukas's ballet *La Péri*, mainly because Natalia Trouhanova, the composer's mistress, had insisted on dancing a minimum number of performances and retaining ownership of the production.[29] He failed to follow through on a number of Calvocoressi's suggestions, leading to "hesitations, disagreements, and delays."[30] Still, what happened to Ravel, second only to Debussy in stature, boggles the mind. Like Debussy, he was courted by Diaghilev early on, and in July 1909 they got to work. Libretti were proposed, with the composer—joined by Diaghilev, Fokine, Bakst, Benois, and Calvocoressi—settling on *Daphnis and Chloë*. An "insane week" followed, with Ravel and Fokine working long past midnight on the libretto. "What complicates things," he wrote to a friend, "is that Fokine doesn't know a word of French and I only know how to swear in Russian."[31] Ravel went to work, but when the new season arrived, he had yet to reach an agreement dividing the royalties with Fokine. There were quibbles over the libretto, and, when the ballet finally went into production in 1912, Diaghilev had transferred his affections to Nijinsky and *Faune*, resulting in a performance that left the composer "in pitiful condition." Even worse, when the ballet premiered in London two years later, Diaghilev, over the

Fig. 8. Claude Debussy (1862–1918), *Jeux*, autograph manuscript, "préparation orchestrale" (pre-orchestral draft), p. 1, April 1913.
The Morgan Library & Museum, New York, Robert Owen Lehman
Collection, on deposit.
↑ **Fig. 9.** Valentine Gross (1887–1968), Drawings of Vaslav Nijinsky's
choreography for *Jeux*, 1913, reproduced in *Comoedia illustré*, 15 June
1913. Fabrice Herrault Collection.

composer's protests, eliminated the chorus, dismissing it as "not only useless but actually harmful," a decision rendered even more egregious because singers were available for the season's operas. Ravel wrote to *The Times* and other newspapers, alerting the public that what it was about to hear was only "a makeshift arrangement" of his original music. The final breach came after the war, when Diaghilev airily rejected *La Valse*, which he hoped to produce during the 1920 season, telling Ravel that it was a masterpiece but not a ballet. The composer picked up his music and left.[32] It's hard to understand what lay behind this sorry history of putdowns, machinations, and bad faith that colored Diaghilev's relations with one of the most distinguished French composers of the era. Why did he feel the need to cut the likes of Debussy and Ravel down to size, and what did he hope to gain by it?

On 25 July 1914 the curtain fell on Diaghilev's grand London season. The dancers and singers scattered. Within a week Europe was at war. As hostilities spread, theaters closed and touring collapsed, with the Ballets Russes likely to follow suit. But Diaghilev was unfazed. With a new artist-lover at his side, Léonide Massine, he viewed the chaos as an opportunity for bold experiments, unhampered by a company and its needs.

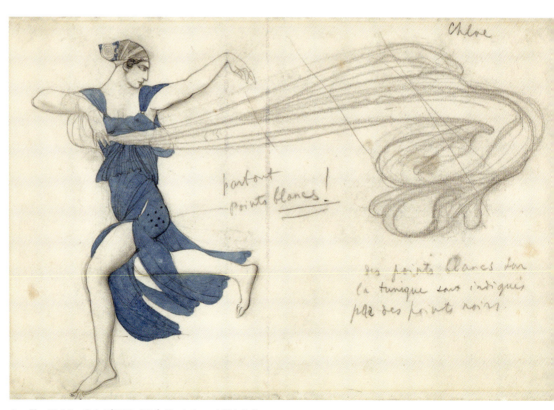

↑ **Fig. 10.** Léon Bakst (1866–1924), *Daphnis and Chloë*, Costume design for Tamara Karsavina as Chloë, 1912. Wadsworth Atheneum, Hartford.
→ **Fig. 11.** Tamara Karsavina in *Daphnis and Chloë*. Camera portrait by E. O. Hoppé. In Valerien Svetlov, *Thamar Karsavina* (London: C. W. Beaumont, 1922). The Morgan Library & Museum, New York.

Futurists had long raised eyebrows, but it was only in the early stages of the war that Diaghilev drew close to this nomadic avant-garde group. The poet Francesco Cangiullo describes a soiree in the Milan drawing room of Filippo Marinetti, the Futurist leader, where Diaghilev presided over a concert of *intuonarumori*—or "noise-intoners"—and Stravinsky was fascinated by the group's "bizarre new instruments." Diaghilev never did present the Futurists in concert in Paris, nor did Stravinsky ever incorporate their instruments into his scores. However, the group descended on Rome to hear him conduct *Petrouchka*, even as Diaghilev went to Naples to explore a Futurist project on the theme of a Neapolitan national holiday.[33] Although only one Futurist collaboration reached the Ballets Russes stage, Diaghilev's contact with the movement altered the company's physiognomy. He said goodbye to naturalism, dramatic narrative, and psychologically motivated characterization. He abandoned the exoticism of Bakst and the retrospectivism of Benois, embracing instead the dynamism, angularity, and studied incongruity of Futurist performance, all of which became trademarks of Ballets Russes modernism.

At the same time Diaghilev was also engaged in a search for old music as a means of creating new scores for ballet. In this he was moving beyond the nineteenth-century concert repertory that Duncan and Fokine had appropriated for dance and the new body of modern music that he had commissioned. Now leaping back to the eighteenth century, he discerned in the lost music of Cimarosa, Pergolesi, and Scarlatti expressions of Latinity's authentic tradition as well as a body of enchanting music all but ignored by dancemakers. The Paris early music scene was particularly active in the years before World War I, and Diaghilev was certainly

aware of it. Benois recounts Diaghilev's enthusiasm for a ballet based on Montéclair's music, and his decision to drop the project because the music had to be played on period instruments. Later, Benois proposed a Bach ballet, but this, too, was scotched when Nijinsky, the proposed choreographer, left the company. However, it is unclear to what extent Diaghilev subscribed to the movement's broader cultural ideas, especially the notion that by "upholding the values of the 'French tradition'—taste (*goût*), balance, brevity, and wit—French composers . . . were resisting German musical hegemony."[34]

Diaghilev's music library, a treasure trove that only came to light in the 1980s when it was auctioned at Sotheby's, testifies to his tenacious research, the care with which he chose and assembled the various pieces of music, and the composers he hired to orchestrate them.[35] The manuscript of *La Boutique Fantasque*, the toyshop ballet that so enchanted London in 1919, raises a question prompted by other composite scores of the period: Who was the author? Rossini, who wrote the early nineteenth-century piano pieces on which the score was based? Respighi, the orchestrator, who added a handful of connectives? Or Diaghilev himself, who assembled the music for the ballet from numerous compositions, pruned bars and passages, changed chords, keys, and tempi, corrected Respighi's additions, and wrote notes to himself like, "Don't forget that all the chords must approximate stylistically the *old* Rossini of *Barber* [*of Seville*]"?[36]

This composite method, closer to a film score in creating an aural support for the action, proved a bonanza for choreographers who sought a particular sound environment for their work or lacked the means to commission new music. Bronislava Nijinska, for instance, cobbled together excerpts from Bach's Brandenburg Concertos for her ballet *Étude* and several pieces by Liszt for *Hamlet*. Years later Balanchine would do the same, assembling musical excerpts by Fauré for *Emeralds* and by Mendelssohn for *A Midsummer Night's Dream*.[37] Ida Rubinstein, who launched her own ballet company in 1928, could well afford to commission new music and did so, Ravel's *Bolero* being among the most notable. However, several of her projects that season, all conceived by Alexandre Benois, were chosen from music by Bach, Tchaikovsky, and the Schubert-Liszt "Soirées de Vienne." In 1920 Stravinsky had created his first composite score, *Pulcinella*, to music by Pergolesi, much of it suggested by Diaghilev. Now in 1928, he composed *Le Baiser de la Fée*, a homage to Tchaikovsky that incorporated more than half of Benois's musical suggestions.[38]

A key aspect of this approach, which I have called "retrospective modernism," is that it juxtaposed modern form and traditional theme or source. Thus *Pulcinella* had designs by Picasso, *La Boutique Fantasque* by Derain; both had choreography by Massine. Although visually Rubinstein's productions revealed the conservativism of Benois's taste, Milhaud's orchestration of the Schubert-Liszt *La Bien-Aimée* (*The Beloved*) had a pianola (which critics mostly decried), while the choreography for the season was almost entirely by Nijinska. If retrospective modernism suggested a way to update period material, its emergence in the mid-1910s also represented an attempt on Diaghilev's part to steer the Ballets Russes away from its Slavic roots, as if exorcizing the loss of Russia—first by war, then by revolution—by replacing it with the vital tradition of classicism. For the British conductor, composer, and critic Constant Lambert, such "time-travelling" led to pastiche becoming "the dominant characteristic of post-war music." Today, he wrote in 1934, "every composer's overcoat has its corresponding hook in the cloakroom of the past."[39] Lambert hated the trend and blamed its ubiquitousness on Diaghilev. The reason, he explained, was that Diaghilev was

> far more than a mere impresario. Though not, strictly speaking, a creative artist, he had very much more genius than many of the artists who worked for

him, and it hardly seems worth while examining the work of such minor composers as Dukelsky, Sauguet, Nabokoff, and others, apart from their association with Diaghileff. They were merely the gunmen executing the commands of their Capone.[40]

Whatever Lambert may have thought, Diaghilev's interest in new music never flagged. He took a personal interest in Sergey Prokofiev, whom he called his "second son," bringing him to Italy, introducing him to Stravinsky, arranging a concert for him in Rome, rejecting the ballet he had brought with him from Russia, then helping him devise the scenario for a new one ("intimate, playful, grotesque, . . . based on a Russian fable"), which eventually became *Chout*. He also engaged him in "three or four passionate and lengthy conversations" about "current tendencies" in the ballet. Diaghilev, Prokofiev wrote in his diary,

> invariably spoke with great heat and conviction. Sometimes his statements would strike you as ridiculous, but it was impossible to object to them because as soon as you tried he would immediately support them with an avalanche of impeccably reasoned theses that would with irrefutable clarity demonstrate the justice of the propositions, however absurd.[41]

Against Diaghilev's wishes, Prokofiev returned to Russia, and the two would not meet again until 1920. *Chout* was going into production, and Diaghilev asked for revisions. He wanted the ballet's six scenes presented without intermission and asked Prokofiev to write the entr'actes; moreover, the whole ballet had to be orchestrated. Prokofiev did not resist. "Diaghilev was a very fine artist," he wrote in his autobiography, "with a thorough knowledge of music." He was also "a subtle and discerning critic. . . . And so we had no difficulty in agreeing on the changes."[42]

Parade was another commission of the war years, a work conceived by the poet Jean Cocteau with music by Erik Satie and designs by Picasso that heralded a new turn in Diaghilev's aesthetic practice. *Parade* was Paris-centered; it was set in the recent past or a present scrubbed of war, and celebrated the sophisticated commonplace. With "acts" inspired by circus, music hall, and cinema, the ballet transformed gentrified populism into modernist artifact. Diaghilev had met Cocteau years before. Satie, however, was a newcomer to his circle. A loner, Satie was the first to reject Wagner's influence on French music; he also rejected impressionism and the "orchestral sonorities" of Debussy and Ravel, seeking instead qualities of "sim-

↑ **Fig. 12.** Mikhail Larionov (1881–1964), Drawing of Serge Diaghilev, Igor Stravinsky, and Sergey Prokofiev, 1921. Harvard Theatre Collection, Houghton Library, Howard D. Rothschild Collection.

plicity, brevity and clarity of expression" that endeared him to the group of young French composers soon to be known as "Les Six."[43] *Parade* itself, despite Cocteau's energetic promotion, never became a repertory standard. However, his collaborators would leave a lasting mark on the Ballets Russes—Picasso, through his designs for nearly a half-dozen productions, and the scores Satie and his musical offspring would contribute to nearly a dozen ballet and opera projects. Finally, with *Parade*, what I have called "lifestyle modernism" entered Diaghilev's world, although its full expression awaited ballets such as *Les Biches* (Poulenc), *Le Train Bleu* (Milhaud), and *La Pastorale* (Auric) in the 1920s. Piquant, amusing, replete with accoutrements of modern living, they belonged to the consumerist chic of a globe-trotting upper class.[44]

In addition to Italy, Diaghilev spent long periods in Spain, which remained neutral throughout the war. Diaghilev "was in ecstasy at the beauty of Spain," his company manager Serge Grigoriev later wrote.[45] From Diaghilev's encounters with the Spanish world in 1916 and 1917 came another cycle of works, of which the most important was *Le Tricorne*, with music by Spain's finest living composer, Manuel de Falla. Falla had spent seven years in Paris before the Great War, leaving only after hostilities began. He was friends with many of Diaghilev's associates, including Calvocoressi, Ravel, and his "idol" Stravinsky, and in 1913 his lyric drama

↑　**Fig. 13.** Pablo Picasso (1881–1973), Design for the front curtain of *Parade*, 1917. Centre Pompidou, Paris.
→　**Fig. 14.** Manuel de Falla (1876–1946), "Farruca" from *Le Tricorne* (*The Three-Cornered Hat*), autograph manuscript, p. 1, July 1918. Dedication to Serge Diaghilev. The Morgan Library & Museum, New York, gift of Robert Owen Lehman, 1972.
→→ **Fig. 15.** Ballets Russes 1919–20 souvenir program with design for *Le Tricorne* by Pablo Picasso from *Collection des plus beaux numéros de "Comoedia illustré" et des programmes consacrés aux ballets et galas russes depuis le début à Paris, 1909–1921*. The Morgan Library & Museum, New York, Mary Flagler Cary Music Collection.

La vida breve was performed at the Opéra-Comique.[46] Back in Spain, Falla worked on a pantomime version of the novella *The Three-Cornered Hat*. For the ballet that Diaghilev now commissioned, he asked Falla to "expand the ending into a fuller, more powerful finale," eliminate some of the "mimetic devices" and "pastiche writing," and transform certain "thematic fragments into full-blown numbers," changes that significantly enhanced the final score. Over the summer of 1917, Diaghilev, Massine, Falla, and the dancer Félix Fernández traveled in slow stages across Castile, Aragon, and Andalusia to gather musical material for the new ballet and "study the infinite variety of native peasant dances." They were a congenial all-male foursome, with Falla, as Massine recalled in his memoirs, "continually writing down passages of music in [his] notebook. . . . He told me that he wanted the dances in the ballet to develop naturally from the story and that he planned to create the whole score anew, enlarging it with new themes, but basing it on his original inspiration."[47] And then they parted. Two years later in London, where Falla traveled for the ballet's premiere, Diaghilev asked him to compose a short introduction to accompany the display of Picasso's enormous drop curtain, proposing an orchestration of "Andaluza," the last of the composer's *Four Spanish Pieces*. Instead, Falla composed a "brief, bombastic evocation of *corrida* . . . music for trumpet, horns, timpani, and voices." Diaghilev also relayed Picasso's suggestion that it would be very Spanish if voices were added not only here but throughout the ballet. Ever the generous collaborator, Falla complied.[48]

On Armistice night 1918, the First World War came to an end. Crowds surged through the streets celebrating the arrival of peace. But for Russians like

Diaghilev who had lived abroad for many years, the rejoicing was muted. In the Russian city of Ekaterinburg less than four months before, the Bolsheviks had executed Nicholas II and his immediate family. The news worsened in 1919, when Diaghilev learned that his beloved stepmother had died after an operation in starving Petrograd (St. Petersburg). In October 1917 the English artist and publisher Charles Ricketts noted in his journal that Diaghilev "wants an Italian revival and a Russian propaganda. We quarreled over German music which he wants to persecute and suppress; he means to scrap Carnaval, Papillons and the Spectre of the Rose"—all with music by German composers.[49] As word reached the West of Bolshevik atrocities, Diaghilev unleashed diatribes in the British press against the "poison gas" of German music. Calling Brahms a "putrefying corpse," Beethoven "a mummy," and Schumann "a homesick dog howling at the moon," he declared that "the influence of Boche culture is more dangerous than even the Boche occupation of Alsace-Lorraine" and that the "vaccine of Boche music [has] all but arrested the development of European music."[50]

Diaghilev never dropped ballets with music by Schumann or Carl Maria von Weber from the repertory. But one can easily view the musical identity of the Ballets Russes in the post-Armistice period as an affirmation of "Latino-Slav art," evident not only in the ballet repertory but also in the "symphonic interludes" that became a feature of Diaghilev's London programming in 1919 and continued intermittently throughout the following decade. Although Russian composers figured prominently in the offerings, the list of French musicians was longer. In 1921 alone, he programmed two of Satie's *Gymnopédies* and his *Trois pièces montées*, Prokofiev's *Symphonie classique*, and music by Ravel, Milhaud, Poulenc, Auric, Chabrier, and Debussy.[51]

Although by now Diaghilev had commissioned a ballet from Poulenc, the project that occupied most of 1921 was *The Sleeping Princess* (as he renamed Petipa's *Sleeping Beauty*), which, despite extensive edits, was as close as Diaghilev ever came to recreating an outstanding example of Maryinsky classicism. For the critic André Levinson, who abhorred Russia's new Bolshevik masters, the revival signified nothing less than the rebirth of St. Petersburg's refined, aristocratic culture. For Diaghilev, it was above all a tribute to "Uncle Petya," as he always called Tchaikovsky, a distant cousin. "I never saw [Diaghilev] work with such ardor and love," wrote Stravinsky decades later. "The moment had at last arrived when he could give to the public a composer whom he had never ceased to love." Hailing "our great and beloved Tchaikovsky" in a letter published in the souvenir program, Stravinsky contrasted his power of melody with the themes and leitmotifs "manufactured" by Germans.[52]

← **Fig. 16.** Henri Matisse (1869–1954), Costume design for *Le Chant du Rossignol* (*The Song of the Nightingale*), 1920. Harvard Theatre Collection, Houghton Library, Howard D. Rothschild Collection.
↑ **Fig. 17.** Pablo Picasso (1881–1973), *Portrait of Igor Stravinsky*, 31 December 1920. Private collection.

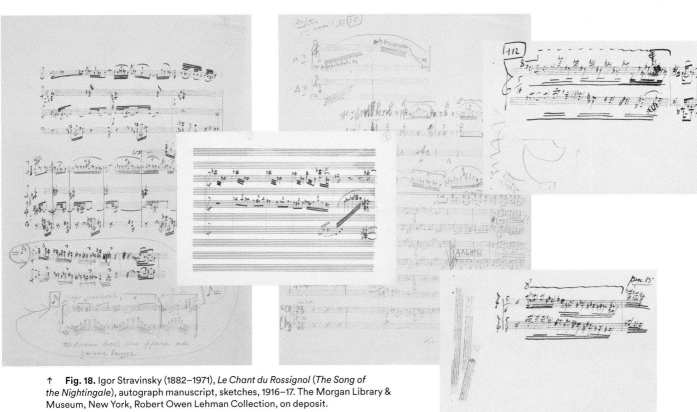

↑ **Fig. 18.** Igor Stravinsky (1882–1971), *Le Chant du Rossignol* (*The Song of the Nightingale*), autograph manuscript, sketches, 1916–17. The Morgan Library & Museum, New York, Robert Owen Lehman Collection, on deposit.

↑ **Fig. 19.** Léon Bakst (1866–1924), Design for the scenery of act III of *The Sleeping Princess*, 1921. The Morgan Library & Museum, New York, gift of Mrs. Donald M. Oenslager, 1982.

The Sleeping Princess was a financial failure, and Diaghilev fled London just ahead of his creditors. Settling in Paris and subsequently Monte Carlo, he steered the company on a French course. To be sure, Stravinsky's opera buffa *Mavra* (based on a Pushkin story), his burlesque pantomime *Le Renard*, and his great dance cantata *Les Noces* premiered in these years, *Les Noces* to great acclaim. Still, most of Diaghilev's new projects were French, as were the composers he now commissioned, and given his relationship with Cocteau they were chiefly from "Les Six." The high point for Diaghilev was the Festival Français, which he organized in Monte Carlo early in 1924, the crux of a plan to insert himself—through the latest metamorphosis of his company's repertory—into an elite French discourse on cultural identity viewed through the prism of the Grand Siècle. As a strategy, retrospective modernism was not new. However, unlike its mainly Italian predecessors, the cycle of retrospectivist operas and ballets that Diaghilev now set out to produce were all French, and all in some way invoked the Grand Siècle. To be sure, only the music by Montéclair for the ballet *Les Tentations de la Bergère*

ou l'Amour vainqueur actually dated to the period. The operas—Gounod's *Philémon et Baucis*, *La Colombe*, and *Le Médecin malgré lui*, and Chabrier's *Une éducation manquée*—all came from the mid-nineteenth century, while the ballet *Les Fâcheux* had a new score by Auric. However, two of the works were inspired by comedies by Molière and two others by tales of his contemporary, the fabulist La Fontaine.

For Diaghilev the journey into the byways of the French musical past became a passion. He spent hours at the Paris Opéra library, studying scores by Auber, Hérold, Rameau, Halévy, Mouret, Mondonville, Destouches, and others; he consulted authorities and had numerous pages copied from old music books. He jotted down titles and dreamed up incongruous pairings: modernist artists such as Larionov for Le Sueur's *Fête à la cour des Miracles*, Derain for *Giselle*, etc.[53] None of these projects came to fruition, but they suggest a counterweight to ballets like *Les Biches*, *Le Train Bleu*, *Les Matelots*, and *La Pastorale*, which were set in the here and now. They also suggest broad differences with the Ballets Suédois, a Paris-based Swedish company founded by Rolf de Maré, which made a splash between 1920 and 1924 with ballets such as *Les Mariés de la Tour Eiffel*,[54] *Skating Rink*, and *La Création du Monde*, all with music by Les Six. History had no place in that company's profile, and few of the dancers saw themselves as part of a ballet lineage. Although *The Sleeping Princess* died at the end of its run, Diaghilev immediately produced *Aurora's Wedding*, a one-act ballet derived from it, and, a few years later, an abbreviated version of *Swan Lake*, underscoring his desire to incorporate his company's pre-Fokine lineage into its identity.[55]

Even at the height of Diaghilev's Latin turn, Russia always remained a presence. In 1920, when he produced Cimarosa's opera-ballet *Le Astuzie Femminili*, Diaghilev relished that it ended with a "Russian ballet." "To me, already head over heels in love with the eighteenth-century Italian music, this final appeal was irresistible," he told *The Observer* before the premiere, noting that in the wedding music Cimarosa "makes use of a tune called 'Kamarinskaia,' a dance which no doubt he saw the peasants dance at weddings in Russia."[56] Diaghilev conceived *Zéphyr et Flore* as a time-traveling Russian serf ballet, telling the twenty-one-year-old composer Vladimir Dukelsky (better known as Vernon Duke), that

← **Fig. 20.** Mikhail Larionov (1881–1964), Costume design for the Fox from *Le Renard*, 1921. Harvard Theatre Collection, Houghton Library, George Chaffee Collection.
↑ **Fig. 21.** Igor Stravinsky (1882–1971), *Le Renard*, autograph manuscript, short score (particell) draft, p. 13, 1916. The Morgan Library & Museum, New York, Robert Owen Lehman Collection, on deposit.

"he wanted a ballet combining classicism with Russian overtones—tutus with *kokoshniks*."[57] Even *Prodigal Son* had a Russian dimension, as Prokofiev noted, Diaghilev's idea being to recast the biblical parable "on to Russian soil."[58] In some works, the Russian subject matter was clear. Nicolas Nabokov's *Ode*, for instance, was at least partly a paean to the eighteenth-century empress Elizabeth Petrovna as was Prokofiev's *Le Pas d'Acier* to the Russian Revolution and its modernization efforts.

To be sure, music by the "Mighty Handful" ebbed, although *Schéhérazade*, the Polovtsian Dances, and *Thamar* were danced throughout the 1920s. But Stravinsky's "Russian" works—*Firebird*, *Petrouchka*, *The Rite of Spring* (with Massine's choreography), and *Les Noces*—were performed with regularity, joined by "neoclassical" works of the composer, such as *Pulcinella* and *Apollon Musagète*. Diaghilev's "first son" bridged both pre- and postwar eras. Prokofiev, his second, and Dukelsky, his third, joined by Nabokov and the teenage Igor Markevitch were Diaghilev's Russian progeny in emigration. (Prokofiev returned to the Soviet Union several years after Diaghilev's death.) Just as in his final years Diaghilev passionately collected rare Russian books, including one by Ivan Fedorov printed in 1564,[59] as testimony to the survival of Russian culture outside the USSR, so he used commissions and mentorship to create a place in emigration for his displaced artists that would allow them to flourish creatively, while retaining their cultural identity.

For the most part, Diaghilev's collaborations of the 1920s were conceived and largely shaped by him. Nabokov has left a hilarious account of how his ambitious mother schemed to bring her son to Diaghilev's notice, in hope of securing a longed-for commission. Once the contact was made, Diaghilev invited him to play his music on the broken-down upright piano in one of the banquet rooms of the Grand Hotel, and then, after the ballet was finished, brought him to Monte Carlo, where he demanded that Nabokov delete a number of "weak" sections and replace them with three new dance movements. Diaghilev was equally high-handed with Dukelsky, admonishing him to "stick to Glinka and Dargomijsky as models and steer clear of Prokofiev," dispatching him and Boris Kochno (the ballet's librettist) to a retreat in the country near Paris to work undisturbed, and following their progress via correspondence. As for Vittorio Rieti, who composed *Le Bal* for the company's last season, Diaghilev had demanded so many changes in the score that when he finally turned it in he wrote: "Here is *Le Bal*. It is dedicated to you; it's yours; do what you want with it, but don't expect me still to work on it."[60]

Year after year, season after season, Diaghilev conceived, commissioned, and produced a steady stream of musical works. Indeed, it is astonishing how many came to fruition. Not all were of the highest quality to be sure, and few seemed destined for a permanent place in the repertory. But they testify to Diaghilev's appetite and ability to oversee every aspect of the composition process, as though, imaginatively, the works that emerged were all his. "I am a barman," he once said. "I have invented . . . a certain cocktail according to a recipe of my own."[61] Not everyone liked the recipe, with its "arbitrary mixture of . . . styles" and dismissive treatment of theme. Although individual works might be witty, they struck many as disposable artifacts—here one season, gone the next. As Cocteau wrote in his libretto for *Le Train Bleu*, "the ballet must go out of fashion in a year."[62]

Diaghilev's "cocktail period" coincided with a rash of commissions to Les Six. French critics hailed his support of French music, but criticized his neglect of other living French composers. Words like "banality" were tossed around, and Milhaud's score for *Le Train Bleu* was dismissed as "music in pyjamas," the latest craze in resort wear.[63] Diaghilev did not pay well, and royalties often reached the composer late. But given the dearth of theatrical commissions for young composers, the opportunity was priceless. "Although the terms proposed by Mr. Diaghilev are hardly favorable to us," wrote Rieti's music publisher in 1925, "I accept them, because I am convinced that it will be of the greatest importance for you as a young composer to have your name appear on Mr. Diaghilev's programs."[64] Georges Auric's biographer credits Diaghilev's three ballet commissions as rekindling his desire to compose.

With the exception of *Les Biches* and *Le Train Bleu*, Diaghilev's cocktail ballets have disappeared. One reason *Les Biches* survived was Poulenc's witty and sophisticated music; another was Nijinska's equally witty and sophisticated choreography. Diaghilev didn't expect this rapprochement to happen, but the moment Poulenc stepped into the studio he and Nijinska clicked. They could barely communicate (Nijinska's French was far from fluent and Poulenc knew no Russian), but they got on famously. "The choreography of *Les Biches* is a masterpiece," Poulenc wrote to the composer Henri Sauguet. "At rehearsals I laugh until I cry," he told Diaghilev.[65] The ballet's "cocktail" origins notwithstanding, composer and choreographer transformed *Les Biches* into a modernist Gesamtkunstwerk.

↑ **Fig. 22.** Bronislava Nijinska as the Hostess in *Les Biches*, 1924.
Library of Congress, Bronislava Nijinska Collection.

To the end, Diaghilev remained a man of music. On his last trip across Europe to Venice, where he died in 1929, he traveled in the company of a young musician, Igor Markevitch, whose career he was launching. They went to Baden-Baden for the music festival and to see Hindemith, then to Munich to hear performances of *The Magic Flute* and *Tristan und Isolde*, where Diaghilev wept. "My sustenance here is Mozart and Wagner," he wrote to Boris Kochno.[66] Salzburg, with *Don Giovanni*, came next. And then, the couple separated, Markevitch to join his mother in Switzerland, and Diaghilev to spend his last days in Venice. He had returned, as Nabokov noted, "to the musical passions of his adolescence,"[67] when the dreams of music-making began but long before he had a glimmer of where they would take him.

↑ **Fig. 23.** Mikhail Larionov (1881–1964), Portrait of Serge Diaghilev, 1929. Harvard Theatre Collection, Houghton Library, Howard D. Rothschild Collection.

NOTES

1   Productions of *Les Noces* were mounted by Ballet West in Salt Lake City (2023) and by the Zurich Ballet (2024). Avatâra Ayuso's *Nijinska: Secreto de la vanguardia* (2023), a new work, was staged by the Ballet de Santiago, Chile.

2   See chap. 11 ("The Problem of Lost Works") in Anna Pakes, *Choreography Invisible: The Disappearing Work of Dance* (New York: Oxford University Press, 2020) for an analysis of the problem.

3   Quoted in Joan R. Acocella, "Vittorio Rieti: An Interview," *Dance Magazine*, January 1982, 77.

4   Nicolas Nabokov, *Old Friends and New Music* (London: Hamish Hamilton, 1951), 66.

5   Quoted in Andrea Olmstead, *Juilliard: A History* (Urbana: University of Illinois Press, 1999), 203. To be sure, Schuman, who composed scores for Martha Graham and Antony Tudor, was largely referring to modern dance.

6   Sjeng Scheijen, *Diaghilev: A Life*, trans. Jane Hedley-Prôle and S. J. Leinbach (London: Profile Books, 2009), 22.

7   Alexandre Benois, *Reminiscences of the Russian Ballet*, trans. Mary Britnieva (London: Putnam, 1941), 166.

8   Israel Nesteev, "Diaghilev's Musical Education," trans. Robert Johnson, in *The Ballets Russes and Its World*, ed. Lynn Garafola and Nancy Van Norman Baer (New Haven: Yale University Press, 1999), 28–29.

9   Marcella Sembrich was a Polish coloratura soprano, Antonio Cotogni an Italian baritone regarded as one of the great male singers of the nineteenth century.

10   Nesteev, "Diaghilev's Musical Education," 33.

11   Ibid., 34; Scheijen, *Diaghilev*, 58.

12   Scheijen, *Diaghilev*, 56.

13   For a list of the operas and ballets produced by Diaghilev, see Lynn Garafola, *Diaghilev's Ballets Russes* (New York: Oxford University Press, 1989), Appendixes B and C; and Garafola and Baer, *The Ballets Russes and Its World*, Appendix ("Operas and Ballets Produced by Serge Diaghilev").

14   Quoted in Nesteev, "Diaghilev's Musical Education," 40. For Diaghilev's music studies, see ibid., 38–40; Scheijen, *Diaghilev*, 55–56, 59–61.

15   V. V. Yastrebtsev, *Reminiscences of Rimsky-Korsakov*, ed. and trans. Florence Jonas, foreword Gerald Abraham (New York: Columbia University Press, 1985), 90. Yastrebtsev, an admirer and friend of the composer, wrote this passage in his 22 September 1894 diary entry.

16   For the exhibition, see John E. Bowlt, "Sergei Diaghilev's 'Exhibition of Historic Russian Portraits,'" in "Sergei Diaghilev and the Ballets Russes: A Tribute to the First Hundred Years," ed. John E. Bowlt and Lynn Garafola, special issue of *Experiment: Journal of Russian Culture* 17 (2011), published by the Institute of Modern Russian Culture/Brill, 76–93.

17   Robert Brussel, "Concert de l'exposition de l'art russe," *Figaro*, 7 November 1906, 3.

18   Robert Brussel, "Un festival de musique russe à Paris," *Figaro*, 16 April 1907, 2. See also Ch. D., "Rimsky-Korsakow à l'Opéra," *Figaro*, 15 May 1907, 5. The adapted works were Balakirev's *Thamar*, Borodin's *Prince Igor*, Liadov's *Baba Yaga*, and Rimsky-Korsakov's *Sadko*. Festival music was incorporated into both *Cléopâtre* and *Le Festin*.

19   Michel Fokine, "The New Russian Ballet," *The Times* (London), 6 July 1914, 6.

20   Jules Claretie, "La Vie à Paris," *Le Temps*, 21 May 1909, 2.

21   Arnold Bennett, "Russian Imperial Ballet at the Opéra," in *Paris Nights and Other Impressions of Places and People* (New York: George H. Doran, 1913), 76–77.

22   M. D. Calvocoressi, *Musicians Gallery: Music and Ballet in Paris and London; Recollections of M. D. Calvocoressi* (London: Faber and Faber, 1933), 76. Born in France of Greek parentage, Calvocoressi was a music critic and translator who wrote extensively about Russian music.

23   By July, Debussy had completed the scenario of *Masques et Bergamasques*, on a commedia dell'arte theme, planned as the first of Diaghilev's French ballets (Edward Lockspeiser, *Debussy: His Life and Mind*, vol. 2 [Cambridge: Cambridge University Press, 1965]), 9. For a description of the scenario, which was published by Durand in 1910, see Appendix C, 262–63.

24   Calvocoressi, *Musicians Gallery*, 221.

25   Igor Stravinsky and Robert Craft, *Conversations with Igor Stravinsky* (New York, 1959; repr. Berkeley: University of California Press, 1980), 46.

26   While undistinguished as a whole, Reynaldo Hahn's *Le Dieu Bleu* inspired some of Bakst's most striking designs. A manuscript of Hahn's is in the Mary Flagler Cary Music Collection of the Morgan Library.

27   Claude Debussy, "Jeux," *Le Matin*, 15 May 1913, 4. Debussy's article, which appeared the morning of the premiere, is translated in Lockspeiser, 266–67.

28   *The Diary of Vaslav Nijinsky*, ed. Romola Nijinsky (London: Victor Gollancz, 1937), 154; *The Diary of Vaslav Nijinsky: Unexpurgated Edition*, ed. Joan Acocella, trans. Kyril FitzLyon (New York: Farrar, Straus and Giroux, 1999; repr. Urbana and Chicago: University of Illinois Press, 2006), 206.

29   For Diaghilev's outrageous behavior, see Lynn Garafola, "The Prewar Careers of Natalia Trouhanova and Ida Rubinstein," in *Legacies of Twentieth-Century Dance* (Middletown, CT: Wesleyan University Press, 2005), 153–54.

30   M. D. Calvocoressi, "Les concerts de danse de Mlle Trouhanowa," *Comoedia illustré*, 15 May 1912, 638.

31   Maurice Ravel to Madame René de Saint-Marceaux, 27 July 1909, in *A Ravel Reader: Correspondence, Articles, Reviews*, ed. Arbie Orenstein (New York: Columbia University Press, 1990), 107.

32   Ravel to M. D. Calvocoressi, 3 May 1910, in Orenstein, *Ravel Reader*, 116; Ravel to Ralph Vaughan Williams, 5 August 1912, and to Jacques Rouché, 7 October 1912, in ibid., 132; "Compositeur et impresario: M. Maurice Ravel contre M. de Diaghilev," *Comoedia*, 18 June 1914, 2; Maurice Ravel, "Protest from M. Ravel," *The Times* (London), 9 June 1914, 9; Arbie Orenstein, "Some Unpublished Music and Letters by Ravel," *The Music Forum*, no. 3 (1973), 315–17; Arthur Gold and Robert Fizdale, *Misia: The Life of Misia Sert* (New York: Knopf, 1980), 227.

33   For Diaghilev's relationship with the Futurists, see Garafola, *Diaghilev's Ballets Russes*, 77–82; for the Neapolitan project, *Sergey Prokofiev Diaries, 1915–1923: Behind the Mask*, trans., annotated, and introd. Anthony Phillips (Ithaca, NY: Cornell University Press, 2008), 24.

34   Carol A. Hess, *Sacred Passions: The Life and Music of Manuel de Falla* (New York: Oxford University Press, 2008), 51. For the Montéclair and Bach projects, see Benois, *Reminiscences*, 349–52. For the relationship between classicism and nationalism in French music and musicological discourse in the decades before World War I, see Scott Messing, "Neoclassicism: The Origins of the Term and Its Use in the Schoenberg/Stravinsky Polemic in the 1920s," Ph.D. diss, University of Michigan, 1986, chap. 1.

35   Materials from Diaghilev's music library came to the Morgan with the Mary Flagler Cary Music Collection in 1968, including orchestral scores and parts for *Firebird* and *Prélude à l'après-midi d'un faune* and the heavily revised version of *Swan Lake* produced by the Ballets Russes in 1911. See the checklist of ballet manuscripts in the back of the present volume.

36   Garafola, *Diaghilev's Ballets Russes*, 92. For a fuller discussion of this, see 90–97. George Dorris uses the term "assembled scores" to describe this phenomenon ("Music on Records: Two Eras of Ballet Music," *Dance Chronicle* 4, no. 2 [1981]: 229–30). "The Music Library of Serge Diaghilev" was sold at Sotheby Parke Bernet, London, on 9 May 1984 ("Ballet

Material and Manuscripts from the Serge Lifar Collection"), lot 157. The sale included a number of other treasures from Diaghilev's collection, including Debussy's manuscript of *Jeux* (lot 149), Poulenc's of *Les Biches* (lot 188), and the joint Satie-Cocteau manuscript of *Parade* (lot 214). A decade earlier, a large collection of musical manuscripts originally assembled by Diaghilev was auctioned in Monte Carlo. The sale included many scores by Cimarosa, Paisiello, Glinka, Grétry, Pergolesi, and Rossini. *The Diaghilev-Lifar Library*, Sotheby Parke Bernet, Monaco, 28–30 November, 1 December 1975, lots 401–59.

37 For *Emeralds* Balanchine used selections from Fauré's *Pelléas et Mélisande* and *Shylock*; for *A Midsummer Night's Dream* Mendelssohn's overture and incidental music to *Ein Sommernachtstraum*, the overture to *Athalie*, the concert overture *Die schöne Melusine*, *Die Erste Walpurgisnacht*, three movements from Symphony no. 9, and the overture to *Die Heimkehr aus der Fremde*. See the entries for both ballets in the Balanchine Catalogue, https://balanchine.org/catalogue-page/catalogue-main-archive/.

38 For the borrowed material in *Le Baiser*, see Richard Taruskin, *Stravinsky and the Russian Traditions: A Biography of the Works through "Mavra,"* vol. 2 (Berkeley: University of California Press, 1996), 1610–13. For the Pergolesi pieces, several of which turned out to be by other composers, see 1463–65 in the same volume.

39 Constant Lambert, *Music Ho! A Study of Music in Decline* (New York: Scribner's, 1936), 63, 67.

40 Ibid., 86.

41 *Sergey Prokofiev Diaries, 1915–1923*, 24.

42 *S. Prokofiev: Autobiography, Articles, Reminiscences*, compiled and ed. S. Shlifstein, trans. Rose Prokofieva (Moscow: Foreign Languages Publishing House, [1959]), 39–40, 56.

43 Robert Orledge, *Satie the Composer* (Cambridge: Cambridge University Press, 1990), 1.

44 For a detailed discussion of *Parade* and lifestyle modernism, see Garafola, *Diaghilev's Ballets Russes*, 98–115.

45 S. L. Grigoriev, *The Diaghilev Ballet, 1909–1929*, ed. and trans. Vera Bowen (London: Constable, 1953), 114.

46 For Falla's years in Paris, see Hess, *Sacred Passions*, chap. 3.

47 Hess, *Sacred Passions*, 111; Léonide Massine, *My Life in Ballet*, ed. Phyllis Hartnoll and Robert Rubens (London: Macmillan/St. Martin's Press, 1968), 115–17. However, as Hess has noted, "the idea that Falla collected new melodies during that tour must be taken cautiously." For instance, the themes of the "Seguidilla," which Massine claims were taken down by Falla, "were intact in *El corregidor y la molinera*," the pantomime on which *Le Tricorne* was largely based. Carol A. Hess, *Manuel de Falla and Modernism in Spain, 1898–1936* (Chicago: University of Chicago Press, 2001), 114.

48 Hess, *Manuel de Falla*, 118, and *Sacred Passions*, 114. *Le Tricorne* was one of many postwar ballets with vocal music. Examples include: *Pulcinella* ("Ballet with Song in One Act"), *Le Astuzie Femminili* ("Opera-Ballet in Three Scenes"), *Cuadro Flamenco* ("Suite of Andalusian Dances"), *Le Renard* ("Burlesque Ballet with Song"), *Les Noces* ("Russian Choreographic Scenes in Four Tableaux"), *Les Biches* ("Ballet with Song in One Act"), and *Ode* ("Spectacles in Two Acts for Chorus, Two Solo Voices, and Symphony Orchestra"). Although Diaghilev largely abandoned opera production in the mid-1910s, he could not abandon the human voice.

49 Quoted in Garafola, *Diaghilev's Ballets Russes*, 93.

50 "Beethoven Idolatry. Mr. Diaghileff Shocked," *The Daily Mail*, 20 May 1919, 5; "German Music: M. Diaghileff's Reply to Mr. [Ernest] Newman," *The Observer*, 1 June 1919, 13.

51 This list has been compiled from the daily playbills in the Princes Theatre file, May–July 1921, Theatre Collection, Victoria and Albert Museum, London. The phrase "Latino-Slav art" is from Hess, *Sacred Passions*, 52.

52 André Levinson, "The Sleeping Princess," in *The Designs of Léon Bakst for "The Sleeping Princess": A Ballet in Five Acts after Perrault* (London: Benn Brothers, 1923), 11–12; Scheijen, *Diaghilev*, 21; Igor Stravinsky, "The Diaghilev I Knew," trans. Mercedes de Acosta, *Atlantic Monthly*, November 1953, 35; "A Letter from Igor Stravinsky," Ballets Russes Souvenir Program: *The Sleeping Princess*, Alhambra Theatre, London, 1921, n.p.

53 Serge Lifar, *Serge Diaghilev: His Life, His Work, His Legend; An Intimate Biography* (New York: G. P. Putnam & Sons, 1940), 230–33.

54 The manuscript of Francis Poulenc's contribution to *Les Mariés de la Tour Eiffel* is in the Morgan Library's Mary Flagler Cary Music Collection.

55 Diaghilev's heavily edited score for his 1911 two-act production of *Swan Lake* is in the Morgan Library's Mary Flagler Cary Music Collection.

56 "Cimarosa at Covent Garden. Italian Opera and Russian Ballet. M. Diaghileff's Theory of Acting," *The Observer*, 20 June 1920, 10.

57 Vernon Duke, *Passport to Paris* (Boston: Little, Brown, 1955), 121.

58 Sergey Prokofiev, 8–28 October 1928, in *Sergey Prokofiev Diaries, 1924–1933: Prodigal Son*, trans. and annotated Anthony Phillips (Ithaca, NY: Cornell University Press, 2021), 729.

59 *Diaghilev-Lifar Library*, lot 182. *Apostol (Acts and Epistles of the Apostles)* was the first book printed in Moscow with the name of place, printer, and time. Fedorov and Peter Mstislavetz were the first named Moscow printers.

60 Nabokov, *Old Friends and New Music*, 61–62, 64, 73; Duke, *Passport to Paris*, 121; Grigoriev, *Diaghilev Ballet*, 253.

61 Arnold L. Haskell, with Walter Nouvel, *Diaghileff: His Artistic and Private Life* (London: Victor Gollancz, 1935), 331. In *Balletomania*, Haskell gives a slightly different version of this: "I am a bar-tender, and have invented certain cocktails. Now other people come and steal my recipes" (Arnold L. Haskell, *Balletomania: The Story of an Obsession* [London: Victor Gollancz, 1934], 183).

62 Fernau Hall, *An Anatomy of Ballet* (London: Andrew Melrose, 1953), 79; Cocteau quoted in Lynn Garafola, *La Nijinska: Choreographer of the Modern* (New York: Oxford University Press, 2022), 172. Two identical typescripts of Cocteau's libretto are in the Bronislava Nijinska Collection, Library of Congress, Music Division, Washington, DC, Box 12, Folder 7.

63 See Garafola, *La Nijinska*, 177–79.

64 Universal-Edition A. G. to Rieti, 24 September 1925, C-20-13.2, Serge Diaghilev Papers, Jerome Robbins Dance Division, New York Public Library for the Performing Arts. For music patronage in France during the interwar period, see Louis K. Epstein, "Toward a Theory of Patronage: Funding for Music Composition in France, 1918–1939," Ph.D. diss., Harvard University, 2013, esp. chap. 4.

65 Colin Roust, *Georges Auric: A Life in Music and Politics* (New York: Oxford University Press, 2020), 77, 88; Poulenc to Sauguet, [November 1923], in *Francis Poulenc: Correspondance 1923–1963*, ed. Myriam Chimènes (Paris: Fayard, 1994), 213, and to Diaghilev, [December 1923], 219. The "reconstruction" of *Le Train Bleu* by Frank Ries for the Oakland Ballet and subsequent restaging for the Paris Opéra Ballet is far from "authentic."

66 Richard Buckle, *Diaghilev* (New York: Atheneum, 1979), 537. See 536–38 for the itinerary.

67 Nabokov, *Old Friends and New Music*, 71.

Crafting the Ballets Russes

Robinson McClellan

↑   **Fig. 1.** Léon Bakst (1866–1924), Set design for bedroom scene for
Schéhérazade, [1910]. Boris Stavrovski Collection, New York.
→   **Fig. 2.** Flyer for Serge Diaghilev's Saison Russe 1910 featuring ballet
"créations" (premieres) including *Schéhérazade* and *Firebird* (*L'Oiseau de Feu*).
The Morgan Library & Museum, New York, James Fuld Collection.

> "If only the painter, the composer, and the choreographer
> would work together in harmony,
> what wonders would they not show the public!"
> —ATTRIBUTED TO JEAN-GEORGES NOVERRE, DANCER AND BALLET MASTER

Crafting the Ballets Russes: Music, Dance, Design—The Robert Owen Lehman Collection is a story of the composers, choreographers, and stage designers who gathered in Paris in 1909, at the height of the Belle Époque, under the leadership of the twentieth century's greatest impresario, Serge Diaghilev. Drawn together by their passionate belief in the transformative power of theatrical art, these kindred spirits sustained a stream of new stage works through twenty years and beyond.

Even before the curtain closed on the Ballets Russes' final season, in 1929, the company embodied a potent cultural legend. These larger-than-life creative figures and the stage works they brought to Europe and the Americas came to be seen as the founders of a revolution in music, dance, art, and fashion. Their legacy comes down in numerous memoirs, interviews, books, and exhibitions, mixing history told in primary documents with oft-repeated tales and anecdotes. The memorable ballets they created established a new, modernist musical repertoire, inspired generations of stage artists, and reimagined what ballet could be, launching the careers of choreographers like George Balanchine, Bronislava Nijinska, and others who built the world of twentieth-century ballet and its leading institutions including the Royal Ballet and the New York City Ballet.

Five main ballets will tell the story, rooted in music manuscripts in the Robert Owen Lehman Collection held on deposit at the Morgan Library: *Firebird* (1910), *Petrouchka* (1911), *L'Après-midi d'un Faune* (1912), *Les Noces* (1923), and *Bolero* (1928). This account follows the creators of these ballets: composers Igor Stravinsky, Claude Debussy, and Maurice Ravel; choreographers Michel Fokine, Vaslav Nijinsky, and Bronislava Nijinska; artists Léon Bakst, Alexandre Benois, and Natalia Goncharova; and Ida Rubinstein, star of Diaghilev's first seasons who became at times his rival as producer. Each ballet was a turning point in the artistic developments of the time, beginning in the ferment of the first years of the Ballets Russes, between 1909 and 1913, following these creators through the 1910s and 1920s as they scattered, and joining them as they later regrouped, this time without Diaghilev, in a new ballet company founded in 1928,

Les Ballets de Madame Ida Rubinstein. Rubinstein's company, though less known than the Ballets Russes, and founded by a woman who is little remembered today, represented the Ballets Russes' chief competition, and embodied new developments in the late 1920s that would come to define ballet for the rest of the twentieth century.

How music, dance, and visual art combined on stage in the hands of these creators, how this new formula electrified audiences, and how the ways in which they conceived and created these works are told in the materials they left us—mainly works on paper: music manuscripts, choreographic notations, and stage designs—are the central threads in this story.

Part 1
How the New Ballet Took Paris

FROM THE MOMENT the Ballets Russes first arrived in Paris, in 1909, led by Serge Diaghilev, the company's trailblazing creations began to spark changes in the staging, presentation, and aesthetics of ballet, and became a prism through which following generations would understand its prestige and influence as an art form. As mentor, arbiter, talent scout, and motivator, Diaghilev reigned over a troupe that continues to cast its influence across music, dance, and design.

Diaghilev brought his troupe to Paris at a propitious moment. At the turn of the twentieth century, ballet was on the decline in France, burdened by outworn repertory, low standards of stagecraft, and a broad belief in the primacy of opera.[1] A seed for ballet's modernist revival was planted with Alexander Benois (1870–1960), a young artist from a family rooted in the arts world of St. Petersburg, when he fell in love with ballet in his childhood (fig. 3). At age twenty, witnessing the 1890 premiere of Piotr Tchaikovsky's *Sleeping Beauty* at the Imperial Ballet Theater, Benois experienced a revelation. In the union of music and dance on stage he perceived a glimmer of something fresh and as-yet unrealized, a spark that could, perhaps, lead beyond the overburdened seriousness of late nineteenth-century Russian art.[2]

Benois gathered a group of young aesthetes in St. Petersburg, meeting for passionate discussions of art, theater, and literature. The group included the artist Léon Bakst (1866–1924), whose stage designs would define the early years of the Ballets Russes (fig. 4), and Serge Diaghilev (1872–1929), a recent arrival from a provincial city, who quickly became the group's leader (fig. 5). With his love of music, unswerving artistic

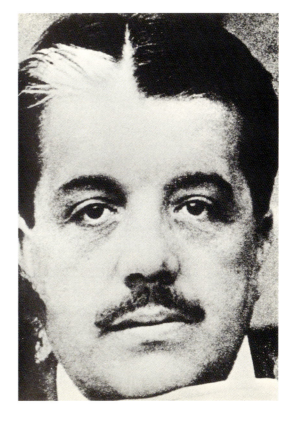

← **Fig. 3.** Konstantin Somov (1869–1939), Portrait of Alexandre Benois, 1908, reproduction. Library of Congress, Bronislava Nijinska Collection.
↑ **Fig. 4.** Léon Bakst (1866–1924), *Self-Portrait*, 1893. State Russian Museum, St. Petersburg.
→ **Fig. 5.** Serge Diaghilev, Lausanne, 1915. Collection of Parmenia Migel Ekstrom.

judgment, and an unmatched talent for logistics, Diaghilev moved the group from theory to practice, mounting art exhibitions and publishing essays. While Benois introduced Diaghilev and the others to his vision of ballet's future potential, other things preoccupied them. They were immersed in the visual arts, and also became, with much of the Western European avant-garde of the time, fervent devotees of Richard Wagner, fascinated by the German composer's dream of the Gesamtkunstwerk, a fusion of art forms on stage.

Between 1898 and 1904 the group published an influential arts journal, *Mir iskusstva* (World of Art) edited by Diaghilev, promoting Russian artists and seeking to bring Russian art up to date with trends from Western Europe, focusing on Symbolist ideals of the artist's autonomy and subjectivity. The logo Bakst created for World of Art, as the group became known, which was used in the group's journal and business correspondence, is an eagle against a starry sky, capturing World of Art's guiding idea that art must remain free, unencumbered by social, religious, philosophical, or ideological demands (fig. 6).

Alexandre Benois kept to his dream of a new ballet. In Russia, ballet had continued to enjoy social prestige under Marius Petipa, the French-Russian ballet master and choreographer who reigned over the Imperial Ballet for three decades, until 1903. The tradition carried forward at St.

↓ **Fig. 6.** Serge Diaghilev (1872–1929), Autograph letter to an unidentified recipient, St. Petersburg, 31 October 1900. *Mir iskusstva* letterhead with illustration by Léon Bakst (1866–1924). The Morgan Library & Museum, New York, James Fuld Collection.

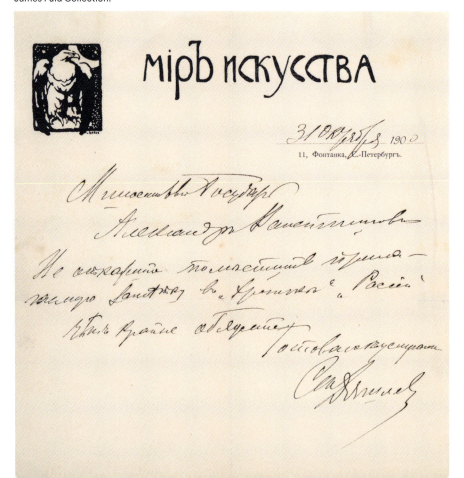

Petersburg's Maryinsky Theater embodied an aristocratic spirit, held over from the prerevolutionary French court of Louis XIV, that remained detached from social and political concerns of late nineteenth-century art as they were expressed in the work of Dostoevsky, Tolstoy, and Mussorgsky. To those who sought after modern artistic progress, Russian ballet appeared as a frivolous aristocratic entertainment, preserved long past its due.

Seeking to revitalize ballet and fulfill the profound artistic and intellectual potential he saw in it, in a 1908 article Benois presented his vision and laid out many of the innovations for which the Ballets Russes would soon become known: the limits of pantomime and the turn toward plotless ballets, the interest in antiquity and Russian folk subjects, the key influence of the innovative American dancer Isadora Duncan, and the need for more inventive use of costumes and décor. Above all, Benois wrote, ballet could transcend opera and spoken drama, both of which were then more dominant. The literary element vital to both—the story, the libretto, the words—could only "fetter" art's freedom, he argued, reducing it to a mundane, earthly level. While operas and plays can make one laugh or cry, ballet offers something far better: being an art of pure gesture, unburdened by the need to represent concrete thoughts and ideas, ballet can bestow the greatest emotion of all: a smile—and not only a smile of the lips, but of the whole body, infusing and elevating the spirit.[3]

AFTER THE JOURNAL *Mir iskusstva* folded in 1904, Diaghilev began planning his "export campaign," as Benois called it,[4] which would become the foundation of the Ballets Russes. At his St. Petersburg apartment Diaghilev gathered the World of Art group, setting his sights on Paris, then the center of the European cultural universe. In 1906 they mounted an encyclopedic exhibition of Russian painting in Paris at the Salon d'Automne, followed in 1907 by "historical concerts" that showcased the leading Russian composers of the day including Nikolai Rimsky-Korsakov, Alexander Scriabin, and Sergei Rachmaninoff. In 1908, at the Paris Opéra, they presented a lavish production of Modest Mussorgsky's *Boris Godunov*, the great Russian opera beloved of French musicians like Debussy and Ravel.

For his next 1909 Paris season, Diaghilev planned a mixed program that would, for the first time, include Russian ballet alongside opera. For some time, he and his colleagues had thought of featuring ballet as it became more clear how well it suited the World of Art's artistic ideals,[5] as Benois expressed them in his 1908 article. To the surprise of Diaghilev and his colleagues, the ballets they presented to Paris in 1909 were more successful with critics than the operas, and they did better financially.[6] For his next Saison Russe in Paris, for June 1910, Diaghilev decided to present ballets exclusively.

LE THÉÂTRE

M. WAZLAW NIJINSKY, PREMIER DANSEUR. — Mlle ANNA PAVLOVA, PRIMA BALLERINA DU THÉÂTRE IMPERIAL MARIE (PÉTERSBOURG)
LE PAVILLON D'ARMIDE

ÉDITEURS : *Manzi, Joyant & Cie, 24, Boulevard des Capucines, Paris.* — PRIX NET : **2** fr.; Étranger, **2** fr. **50**

↑   **Fig. 7.** Vaslav Nijinsky and Anna Pavlova in *Le Pavillon d'Armide*, a ballet with scenario and designs by Alexandre Benois. Special issue of *Le Théâtre* devoted to the 1909 Saison Russe, no. 249, May 1909.

→   **Fig. 8.** Valentin Serov (1865–1911), Portrait of Michel Fokine. Reproduced in the *Comoedia illustré* souvenir program for the 6–7 June 1911 Ballets Russes season at the Théâtre du Châtelet, Paris. The Morgan Library & Museum, New York, James Fuld Collection.

The World of Art continued to pursue the dream of a synthesis or fusion of the arts on stage, harking back to the ideal of the Gesamtkunstwerk, or "total artwork," most famously envisioned in 1849 by the German composer Richard Wagner. It was a topic much discussed in Belle Époque Paris and promoted in publications like the *Revue wagnérienne*, and it informed the expectations of the Ballets Russes' first audiences.[7] A vital ingredient was the group of star dancers from the Imperial Ballet at the Maryinsky Theater in St. Petersburg, including Anna Pavlova, Vaslav Nijinsky, and Tamara Karsavina (fig. 7).[8] Raised in the world of classical ballet at the Imperial Ballet School, these dancers brought revolutionary leanings and an appetite for something new.

Michel Fokine (1880–1942), a young dancer and rising choreographer at the Maryinsky Theater, shared with the World of Art a strong interest in the Gesamtkunstwerk ideal (fig. 8). He became a key creative force in the Ballets Russes when Diaghilev made him the choreographer for the company's first, defining seasons in Paris. In a 1914 letter to the London *Times* he captured a set of principles that had, in his view, defined the troupe's creative approach: among these was "... the alliance of dancing with the other arts." The new ballet, he wrote, would not be subjugated to the demands of the music or design, but would recognize "the alliance of the arts only on the condition of complete equality."[9]

The American dancer Isadora Duncan, whose performances were popular in Europe from the turn of the twentieth century, played a key role in shaping Fokine's vision for ballet. Her appearances in St. Petersburg beginning in 1904 made an enormous impression on Diaghilev and his World of Art colleagues. Her use of ancient Greek sources helped to inspire Léon Bakst's interest in antiquity (see figs. 24–26), and her new style of dance, while representing a departure from ballet rather than a reform, made a powerful impact on Fokine's choreography and artistic vision. His work with the Ballets Russes helped to project key aspects of Duncan's innovations through twentieth-century ballet, opening, as Lubov Blok put it, "a whole universe of new possibilities: one could explore new directions, elicit dance images from ... symphonic music, inhabit one's free dancing body without feeling the constraints of real or imaginary convention. Even more important, one could be serious about dance, think of it not as an amusement or a form of theater, but as one would think of music."[10] These revelatory new approaches, manifest in Duncan's and Fokine's work, were significant in the transformation of the World of Art into the Ballets Russes.

Schéhérazade, which premiered in June 1910 at the Paris Opéra, Palais Garnier starring Ida Rubinstein and Vaslav Nijinsky, was the first original ballet Diaghilev and his col-

M. Fokine
l'éminent maître de ballet, directeur chorégraphique de la Troupe Russe

leagues created specifically for Paris (fig. 9); the others had been adapted from previous productions from St. Petersburg. This ballet seemed to fulfill the potential in the Gesamtkunstwerk ideal, in all its dreamed-of glory. Fusing sound, color, and movement into a single sensuous experience, the ballet offered a spectacle unlike any Paris audiences had witnessed before. Bakst's designs for *Schéhérazade* made an enormous impact on the city, influencing fashion and design beyond the theater.[11] Together, the elements of the ballet, invoking an imagined Persia—Rimsky-Korsakov's exoticized music, Fokine's dance full of violence and sexual debauchery, and Bakst's mind-bending juxtapositions of color and line (see fig. 1)— made the ballet an emblem of the Orientalist fervor that gripped Europe, and today encapsulates the era's deep history of racial caricature and exclusion (see pp. 60–61).

DIAGHILEV'S 1910 PARIS season brought another new requirement: music better suited to modern French tastes. While French critics had adored the ballets' choreography and set designs the previous year, they had found the music, written by a lineup of current Russian composers, lacking the freshness of the other elements.[12] Following his 1909 season, Diaghilev approached leading French composers including Gabriel Fauré, Maurice Ravel, and Claude Debussy, convincing Debussy to begin work on a new ballet for the next year.[13] But when those projects were canceled or delayed, the impresario decided to take a risk on a little-known composition student in St. Petersburg: Igor Stravinsky (1882–1971), commissioning a ballet for 1910—though only after passing over at least three other composers.[14]

Diaghilev also took a risk on what was then, perhaps surprisingly, a new subject for a Russian ballet: Russia. Though ballet had thrived in Russia through the nineteenth century, it remained primarily a Western-identified art form. Originally imported from France, the tradition at the Imperial Ballet retained its French character, seen in the subjects and titles of the ballets brought from the Maryinsky Theater and premiered in the 1909 Paris season such as *Le Pavillon d'Armide*—based on a story by the French Romantic poet and critic Théophile Gautier with set designs by Benois showcasing his deep knowledge of the court of Louis XIV at Versailles (see fig. 7). But Parisians of the Belle Époque clamored for anything that suggested the exotic, which for them included Russia. And so, in an odd reversal, Russian ballet now had to become more "Russian" to suit its French audience. Diaghilev's group cast around for a suitable subject and settled on a popular character from Russian folklore, never used in a ballet before: the Firebird.

An informal committee took on the task of creating the story, although the libretto is credited to Fokine. The narrative is simple and

↑ **Fig. 9.** Jacques-Émile Blanche (1861–1942), Ida Rubinstein as Zobéide in *Schéhérazade*, ca. 1910. Harvard Theatre Collection, Houghton Library, Howard D. Rothschild Collection.

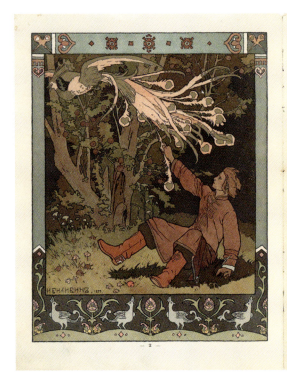

↑↑ **Fig. 10.** Ivan Bilibin (1876–1942), Illustration from *Skazka ob Ivane-tsareviche, Zhar-ptitse i o serom volke* [Tale of Ivan-Tsarevich, the Firebird, and the Grey Wolf], from the series "Skazki" [Folk tales] by Alexander Afanasyev, pp. 2–3 (St. Petersburg: Ekspeditsiya zagotovleniya gosudarstvennikh bumag, 1901). The Morgan Library & Museum, New York, purchased on the Elisabeth Ball Fund, 1992.

↑ **Fig. 11.** Igor Stravinsky (1882–1971), "Adagio / Supplication of the Firebird" from *Firebird*, autograph manuscript, piano, extensive revisions, pp. 11–12, [1910], inscribed 1918. The Morgan Library & Museum, New York, Robert Owen Lehman Collection, on deposit.

full of folkloric touches: a daring prince, Ivan Tsarevich, battles the evil wizard Koschei. With the Firebird's help, and a magic egg, he wins the beautiful Tsarevna (fig. 10). For Russians, the story was a silly hodge-podge. But *Firebird* was not meant for them. It was for Paris, designed expressly for export.

Igor Stravinsky labored furiously over the score during the early months of 1910, composing at the piano (fig. 11). Almost from the beginning, he worked closely with Fokine. The choreographer, the more experienced and better known of the two, was firmly in charge. As Fokine recalled,

> I did not wait for the composer to give me the finished music. Stravinsky visited me with his first sketches and basic ideas.... At my request, he broke up his national themes into short phrases corresponding to the separate moments of a scene, separate gestures and poses.... Stravinsky played, and I interpreted the role of the Tsarevich, the piano substituting for the wall. I climbed over it, jumped down from it, and crawled, fear-struck, looking around—my living room. Stravinsky, watching, accompanied me with patches of the Tsarevich melodies, playing mysterious tremolos as background to depict the garden of the sinister Immortal Kostchei ... and so on.[15]

Rehearsals began in March in St. Petersburg. Serge Grigoriev, the Ballets Russes rehearsal director, recalled how "Stravinsky was usually present to indicate the tempo and rhythms. Now and again he would play over passages himself and, according to some of the dancers, 'demolish the piano.' He was particularly exacting about the rhythms and used to hammer them out with considerable violence, humming loudly and scarcely caring whether he struck the right notes."[16]

↑ **Fig. 12.** Rehearsal at the Catherine Hall, St. Petersburg. Igor Stravinsky at the piano; Michel Fokine standing in white jacket, referencing notes; Tamara Karsavina at right.

For *Firebird*'s stage designs, Diaghilev hired Alexander Golovin, whose scenery for the 1908 production of *Boris Godunov* had been well received. The impresario was, however, unhappy with Golovin's costumes for the Firebird and Tsarevna characters, and asked Léon Bakst to recast them.[17] Many details of Bakst's 1910 and 1913 designs for the Firebird costume match closely—the double braids, flying attachments to the headdress and skirt, and tear-shaped medallion (figs. 13, 14). The same features are evident in a 1910 photograph of the costume worn by Tamara Karsavina, the ballerina who created the role in the original production (fig. 16).

Comparing drawings with photographs can reveal the ways in which stage designs are mediated by those who make the sets and costumes—just as the ideas of composers and choreographers are interpreted by musicians and dancers. Designs by Bakst and others often lacked much practical information—here, for example, showing only the front of the costume—and costume makers took considerable freedom in interpreting them.[18] At the same time, in Ballets Russes performances the movement on stage revealed bare flesh and fantastical shapes, perhaps coming closer, for the audience, to the impressions given in Bakst's drawings.[19]

Bakst's 1915 drawing for *Firebird* was probably made not as a costume design but for a poster to advertise the Ballets Russes' 1916 tour to North America (fig. 15). The floating poses and flying garments, with sexual overtones, make clear that this was an image intended to draw the viewer's attention.

↑ **Fig. 13.** Léon Bakst (1866–1924), Costume design for *Firebird*, 1910. Private collection.
→ **Fig. 14.** Léon Bakst (1866–1924), Costume design for *Firebird*, 1913. The Museum of Modern Art, New York, the Joan and Lester Avnet Collection.

AT *FIREBIRD*'S PREMIERE at the Paris Opéra, Stravinsky's music received an enthusiastic response. While aspects of the score are indebted to his teacher Nikolai Rimsky-Korsakov, Stravinsky's masterful orchestration, and his use of Russian folk music that was subtler and deeper than his teacher's, set it apart.[20] Whatever combination of Diaghilev's famously canny intuition and pure luck allowed the impresario to win his bet on this young composer, the future was clear: Stravinsky was an instant star, and became a core member of Diaghilev's creative team. For the first time, *Firebird* brought music up to the same level as the choreography and stage designs. Diaghilev and his World of Art colleagues felt they had achieved the Gesamtkunstwerk of their dreams, Wagner's vision as they reimagined it: three art forms fused within a single, stunning experience—like *Schéhérazade*, with music now playing an equal role.

← **Fig. 15.** Léon Bakst (1866–1924), Poster design for *Firebird*, "Firebird and the Prince (Tsarevitch)," 1915. Harvard Theatre Collection, Houghton Library, Howard D. Rothschild Collection.

↑ **Fig. 16.** Tamara Karsavina and Michel Fokine in *Firebird*, 1910. Library of Congress, Bronislava Nijinska Collection.

WHILE IT IS impossible to define precisely what excited the Ballets Russes' audiences so much, it is clear that something made these ballets different. Although many adulatory eyewitness accounts date from later decades when the legend of the Ballets Russes had reached its full bloom, perhaps coloring their reliability, there are contemporary accounts, like those by Count Harry Kessler, a German diplomat who was well-informed in the artistic trends of the day, that offer a sense of the strong impression Diaghilev's company made on its first audiences. "Since seeing [Richard Wagner's opera] *Tristan [und Isolde]* for the first time," Kessler wrote in 1909, "I don't think I've ever been so deeply impressed by a theatrical production. . . . These women ([Anna] Pavlova, [Tamara] Karsavina, [Ida] Rubinstein), and these men, or rather, boys, [Vaslav] Nijinsky and a few others, seem to have descended from another, higher, more beautiful world, like young living gods and goddesses. . . . We are truly witnessing the birth of a new art."[21]

It was not that the individual elements were new. The designs of Bakst, Benois, and other Ballets Russes artists were not in themselves markedly different from those seen in many theaters of the time—though it was unusual that they sought a unified visual concept for each ballet.[22] Likewise, Fokine's choreography and Stravinsky's music were not alone in their excellence. Even the concept of artistic synthesis, expressed in Wagner's Gesamtkunstwerk ideal, had interested Europe's artistic world since the 1850s, and the fascination with ancient Greek drama and its blending of art forms went back to the Renaissance and the rise of opera since the seventeenth century. What made these Russian ballets feel so new and potent was, perhaps, the way Diaghilev and his creative teams turned familiar artistic vocabularies to new purpose, and the extreme care with which the composers, choreographers, and artists coordinated every detail of the productions, giving thought to how the elements would combine on stage, music, dance, and design—each of the highest quality, each contributing equally, blending as a unified artistic vision.

Music and Dance Notations for *Firebird*

Stravinsky was known for his physical connection to the piano as a fundamental aspect of his compositional process, writing that "fingers are . . . great inspirers, and, in contact with a musical instrument, often give birth to subconscious ideas which might otherwise never come to life."[23] The black and red markings of his piano manuscript for *Firebird* offer a vivid record of the working relationship between Stravinsky and Fokine, showing how the composer followed the choreographer's creative lead (see p. 49). Fokine was musically skilled, having composed and orchestrated arrangements of folk music, informing his part in the collaboration.[24]

Their close collaboration is particularly evident where Stravinsky has crossed out, rewritten, or moved music to other parts of the ballet; since many passages would have worked well musically as they were, the changes appear to show him following Fokine's preferences.[25] Stravinsky had opinions too. The ballerina Tamara Karsavina, who created the role of the Firebird in 1910,[26] remembered the strong wills involved and how Diaghilev played his frequent role as arbiter in the creative process: "Stravinsky and Fokine . . . appealed to Diaghilev in every collision over the tempi"[27]—tempo being an area in which the composer had particularly strong feelings.[28]

The Lehman Collection also includes an early published edition of the score with the composer's revisions, some of which may reflect Fokine's influence.[29] The final page contains Stravinsky's extensive changes to the musical meter in the concluding coronation scene,[30] shown here next to the same passage from the manuscript (which bears his

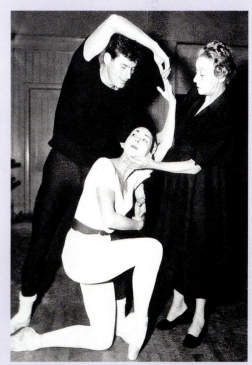

completion date: 21 March 1910, three days after rehearsals had begun). This was one of the few places where a scenic idea of Stravinsky's own prevailed, replacing the divertissement that Fokine had envisioned.[31]

Compared with the importance of music notation in the creation, conception, and memory of a musical work, choreographic notation plays a far lesser role in dance composition. Creation and transmission are ephemeral, flowing mainly through direct contact, in body and voice, as in this photograph showing Tamara Karsavina at age seventy teaching the Firebird role to the ballerina Margot Fonteyn. Dance notation, if used at all, serves mainly as a memory aid, often made after the fact to describe, rather than to prescribe, the performed result—as music notation is designed to do.[32]

OPPOSITE TOP: Igor Stravinsky (1882–1971), End of the final tableau from *Firebird*, autograph manuscript, piano, p. 43, [1910], inscribed 1918. The Morgan Library & Museum, New York, Robert Owen Lehman Collection, on deposit.

OPPOSITE BOTTOM: Igor Stravinsky (1882–1971), "The Enchanted Garden of Koschei" and opening of "Appearance of the Firebird, Pursued by Prince Ivan" from *Firebird*, autograph manuscript, piano, extensive revisions, p. 3, [1910], inscribed 1918. The Morgan Library & Museum, New York, Robert Owen Lehman Collection, on deposit.

ABOVE: Igor Stravinsky (1882–1971), End of the final tableau from *Firebird*, first edition of the score, numerous annotations and revisions in the composer's hand (Moscow: P. Jurgenson, [n.d.]). The Morgan Library & Museum, New York, Robert Owen Lehman Collection, on deposit.

RIGHT: Tamara Karsavina and Michel Fokine in *Firebird*, 1910. Reproduced in *Collection des plus beaux numéros de "Comoedia illustré" et des programmes consacrés aux ballets et galas russes depuis le début à Paris, 1909–1921*. The Morgan Library & Museum, New York, Mary Flagler Cary Music Collection.

FAR RIGHT: Tamara Karsavina (at right) teaching the role of the Firebird to Margot Fonteyn, with Michael Somes, for a revival by the Sadler's Wells Ballet, Edinburgh, 1954.

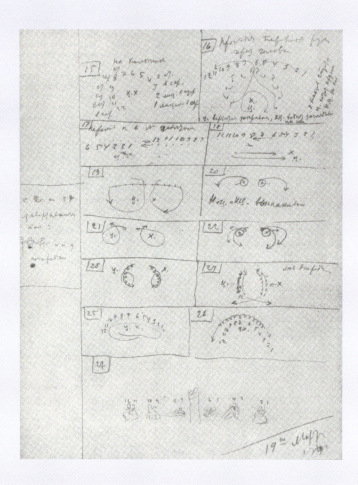

Still, Fokine's choreographic notations for *Firebird* offer a meaningful view into his creative concept for the ballet. In these floor path drawings he identifies two lead dancers with "x" and "y" (it is not clear which characters they represent), and the Enchanted Princesses with numbers 1–12. The numbered boxes, 1 to 27, show specific moments in the dancers' movement across the stage. In the final box, 27, Fokine zooms in with more detail, sketching stick figures to convey arm positions and poses, showing how he switches between different modes as required for the purpose at hand.[33]

Fokine wrote of the innovations he introduced: "In place of acrobatic tricks designed to attract applause, and formal entrances and pauses made solely for effect, there shall be but one thing—the aspiration for beauty. Through the rhythms of the body,

ballet can find expression for ideas, sentiments, emotions. The dance bears the same relation to gesture that poetry bears to prose. Dancing is the poetry of motion."[34]

Dance is at once a musical and visual art. It joins the rhythmical aspects it shares with music—manifest both in sound and movement of the body— with the visual aspects it shares with art—color and shape. Dance was well suited to serve at the center of a new Gesamtkunstwerk, a union of arts onstage. As Alexandre Benois wrote in July 1910, shortly after *Firebird*'s premiere, "In ballet . . . one is all the time in what I would call the elements of united visual and auditory impressions—in ballet the ideal Gesamtkunstwerk is achieved about which Wagner dreamed."[35]

Michel Fokine (1880–1942), *Against the Tide: Memoirs of a Ballet Master*, Choreographic notations for *Firebird*, reproduced on pp. [260–61] (Leningrad: Iskusstvo, 1962). Private collection, New York.

In *Petrouchka*, presented to Paris the following 1911 season, the World of Art group perceived its greatest creation yet. As with *Schéhérazade* and *Firebird*, audiences were struck by the way *Petrouchka* fused music, dance, and design. It seemed, wrote Prince Peter Lieven, a friend of Benois, "as if a single super-genius, equally gifted in music, art, painting and choreography, had conceived, devised, and staged this ballet."[36]

Where Fokine's choreography had guided Stravinsky's music in *Firebird*, in *Petrouchka* the music came first, leading the visual design and choreography. At the time, this was a radical aspect of the ballet:[37] a key legacy of Diaghilev's Ballets Russes was that music became the guiding art within the trinity of music, dance, and design, newly elevating the role of the ballet composer.

Firebird made Stravinsky famous; *Petrouchka* made him *Stravinsky*, honing the startling new musical voice that would define many of his works to come.[38] His distinctive sound can be heard particularly in his novel approach to Russian folk music. Musicologist Richard Taruskin recounts the way Stravinsky went far beyond the popular nineteenth-century practice of borrowing from folk tunes, studying sources with "precise ethnographic observation." The composer integrated traditional Russian idioms into a musical language that felt fresh to its first audiences, securing his status as a leading modernist.[39] His distinctive approach to rhythm became one of the defining aspects of Stravinsky's music: pounding beats, sudden disjunctures, frequent changes of meter, and extensive use of syncopation. The full orchestral manuscript of 1911 (fig. 17) show-

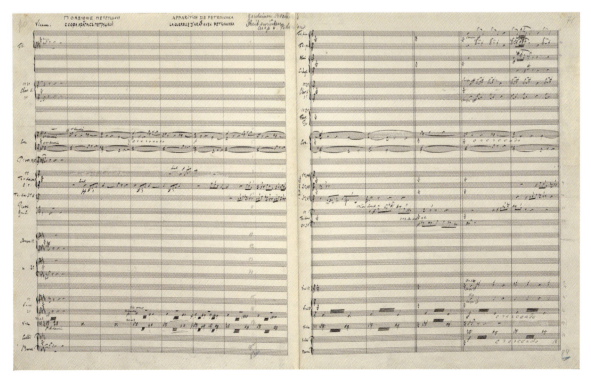

↑ **Fig. 17.** Igor Stravinsky (1882–1971), *Petrouchka*, autograph manuscript, full score, pp. 70–71, 26 May 1911. The Morgan Library & Museum, New York, Robert Owen Lehman Collection, on deposit.

cases the composer's elegant, calligraphic hand, and is one of the few surviving sources for the ballet from the period of its creation.[40]

Belying the sense of artistic cohesion *Petrouchka* projected on stage, the ballet's process of creation was initially haphazard. Following *Firebird*'s success, there was talk of a new Stravinsky ballet based on Edgar Allen Poe's *Masque of the Red Death*.[41] But when Diaghilev approached him to discuss plans for the new work, the composer confessed that he had already begun work on his next Russian-themed ballet, collaborating with the designer, archaeologist, and philosopher Nicholas Roerich.[42] The new ballet, which he was then calling "The Great Sacrifice," would become *The Rite of Spring* (*Le Sacre du Printemps*), his most famous work since its notorious 1913 premiere (see Garafola fig. 7).

In the meantime, another project intervened. By June 1910, around the time of *Firebird*'s premiere, Stravinsky had already begun work on a concert piece for piano and orchestra. He imagined the piano acting as an impudent puppet, a character drawn from street fairs of old Russia, who would interrupt the orchestra.[43] When Diaghilev heard Stravinsky's early drafts in October that year, he understood its potential as a ballet, and recruited Alexander Benois to work with the composer.[44]

Benois's contribution to *Petrouchka* is fundamental, and he is accurately listed as co-author of the ballet in playbills and editions of the score.[45]

His ideas lay at the center of the ballet's scenario: merging Stravinsky's initial inspiration, the stock Petrushka character with his squawking voice and aggressive antics (the English version of this character is Punch, of Punch and Judy) with Pierrot, the sad clown with painted face, loose white costume, and pointed hat, from the seventeenth-century commedia dell'arte tradition interpreted through the lens of Symbolism.[46] The ballet's central character, the forlorn puppet in love with the Ballerina who is enamored of the Moor, becomes a Pierrot, remaining "Petrouchka" in name only. The story evokes a historical time and place Benois loved: an old-fashioned "Butter Week" fair of St. Petersburg in the 1830s, the days of his parents' generation.[47] Benois's vivid designs for *Petrouchka* drew on his childhood memories of such fairs and featured a large cast of characters from every walk of Russian life (fig. 18). Tamara Karsavina, who created the role of the Ballerina, wrote that "it was an essential feature of Benois that he not merely reconstituted an epoch, but invested it with weird, irresistible power over one's imagination."[48]

Fig. 18. Alexandre Benois (1870–1960), Set design for the Butter Week Fair for *Petrouchka*, scenes 1 and 4, 1911. Wadsworth Atheneum, Hartford.
↑   Fig. 19. Dover Street Studios (London, active ca. 1906–ca. 1912), Vaslav Nijinsky as Petrouchka. Library of Congress, Ida Rubinstein Collection.

Michel Fokine's contribution proved equally vital to the effect. Keeping to the first of the five principles he would publish in his 1914 letter to the London *Times*, to "create in each case a new form corresponding to the subject, the most expressive form possible for the representation of the period and the character of the nation represented,"[49] Fokine showed the versatility of his method in its ability to portray, equally vividly, in one instance a magical Firebird and in another a tragic clown amid a large crowd of distinct characters, each highly individualized (see fig. 18). Although his choreography for *Petrouchka* came after the score and scenario were already complete, the effect on stage was a convincing synthesis. As Fokine wrote later, "one could call it a musico-dramatic composition by Stravinsky which assumed an exceptionally important place in the field of modern music; and one could say that it was one of the greatest works of Benois . . . [or] a Fokine production which was one of the most complete demonstrations of his application of ballet reforms."[50]

Vaslav Nijinsky's portrayal of the doomed puppet (fig. 19) was one of his most striking and beloved roles. As Stravinsky wrote,

to call [Nijinsky] a dancer would only be half of the truth, because to an even greater degree he was a dramatic actor. His face, not classically beautiful but fine and expressive, could turn into a mask, a mask which impressed me more than any other actor's mask I have ever seen. In the part of Petrouchka he has created the most pathetic image that has ever appeared before me on the stage.[51]

Like *Firebird*, *Petrouchka* became part of the Ballets Russes' core repertory. The ballet cemented Stravinsky's role as a key member of Diaghilev's personal and artistic entourage.[52]

The Golden Slave and the "Arab": Stories Lost and Distorted

While the events told here are true to every possible extent, this remains an incomplete history, privileging dominant social groups and limited perspectives. Racist representation pervades the works of the Ballets Russes and the culture of its time. The Golden Slave, the virtuosic role danced by Vaslav Nijinsky in the 1910 ballet *Schéhérazade*, set in Persia, is feminized and emasculated: key aspects in Edward Said's analysis of Orientalism's distorted representations. In Ida Rubinstein's role in *Schéhérazade* as Queen Zobéide, antisemitic allusions to her appearance and name underlined the racialized exoticism, coupled with eroticism, that titillated Paris audiences of the Belle Époque.[53] A short 1926 biography of Rubinstein blends *Schéhérazade*'s original, quasi-Persian evocations into a misleading, but tellingly racialized, description of the Golden Slave, inaccurately recalling the ballet's costumes and dancing when Queen Zobéide "charms the beast and smiles at the risks of the bite," caressing "the frizzy head, the muscular neck."[54]

French critics framed the Ballets Russes' success in terms of the troupe's own perceived racial and cultural "otherness," conceiving the Russian body as profoundly different from the French.[55] Reviews frequently described the dancers as "intoxicating," "wild," and "barbaric" (*grisant*, *sauvage*, *barbare*).[56]

ABOVE: George Barbier (1882–1932), *Schéhérazade: Queen Zobéide and the Golden Slave* [performed by Ida Rubinstein and Vaslav Nijinsky in the 1910 premiere], 1913.

RIGHT: Alexandre Benois (1870–1960), "Arap," in *Azbuka v kartinakh* [Alphabet in Pictures] (Saint Petersburg: Expedition of State Papers, 1904). The Morgan Library & Museum, New York, purchased on the Elisabeth Ball Fund, 1992.

FAR RIGHT: *Collection des plus beaux numéros de "Comoedia illustré" et des programmes consacrés aux ballets et galas russes depuis le début à Paris, 1909–1921*. The Morgan Library & Museum, New York, Mary Flagler Cary Music Collection. On left: Stravinsky "Author" and Nijinsky "Interpreter" of *Petrouchka*; right: Alexander Orlov in *Petrouchka*, 1911.

When Stravinsky and Benois imagined the role of the Moor in *Petrouchka*—the villain who battles the puppet for the love of the Ballerina—they drew the character from an illustrated Russian alphabet book Benois had made for his children, in which the letter "A" introduces the "Arap" (Arab). Stravinsky used the same moniker in his score for the scene "The Quarrel of the Arab with Petrouchka" (see fig. 17), and the character was danced in blackface by Alexander Orlov in the first performance in 1911, a practice now widely understood to be deeply offensive.[57]

New approaches have been tried in more recent performances of *Petrouchka* and other ballets to avoid the use of blackface and other debasing caricatures.[58] More broadly, vital work is being done by artists like Kandis Williams to interrogate racist currents in classical ballet.[59] However, the legacy endures as a deeply rooted part of the Western art tradition.

IF IGOR STRAVINSKY and Vaslav Nijinsky were among Diaghilev's great discoveries in those first Paris seasons, another was Ida Rubinstein (1883–1960), a young woman from a prosperous St. Petersburg family. She had mounted productions of Sophocles's *Antigone* in 1904 and Oscar Wilde's *Salomé* in 1908 in St. Petersburg, collaborating with Bakst and Fokine before they came to Paris with Diaghilev. Her sensual, riveting lead performances with the Ballets Russes in *Cléopâtre* (1909) and *Schéhérazade* (1910; see pp. 47, 60) helped secure the company's early reputation. Diaghilev sought to engage Rubinstein in subsequent seasons, offering her roles in *Thamar* (1912)[60] and *L'Après-midi d'un Faune* (1912).[61] But Rubinstein did not see her future as a mere member of Diaghilev's troupe. After the Italian poet Gabriele D'Annunzio saw Rubinstein in *Schéhérazade*, he invited her to collaborate on *The Martyrdom of St.*

↑ **Fig. 20.** *Comoedia illustré: numéro spécial*, vol. 3, no. 17, 1 June 1911. The Morgan Library & Museum, New York, Mary Flagler Cary Music Collection, purchased 2022. On left: Léon Bakst (1866–1924), Illustration for Ida Rubinstein as St. Sebastian in *The Martyrdom of St. Sebastian*; right: The composer Claude Debussy, poet Gabriele D'Annunzio, and artist Léon Bakst, 1911.

Sebastian (*Le Martyre de Saint Sébastien*), a staging of the life of St. Sebastian, the third-century Christian martyr. Starring in the title role as the male saint, she commissioned a new score from Claude Debussy, whom Diaghilev had attempted to hire for the Ballets Russes in 1909, and borrowed two of the impresario's key talents: Léon Bakst created stunning designs, including Rubinstein's costumes (fig. 20), and Michel Fokine choreographed the dance sequences. *The Martyrdom of St. Sebastian* premiered in May 1911 at the Théâtre du Châtelet,[62] the same Paris venue where Diaghilev would present *Petrouchka* just two weeks later. It was the first of many works Rubinstein would produce and star in over the next three decades.

The year 1911 also saw the departure of Diaghilev's longtime collaborator and friend, Alexandre Benois. After a series of disagreements, the artist left the Ballets Russes, returning to Russia where, following the 1917 Revolution, he served as curator and director of St. Petersburg's Hermitage Museum and as repertory adviser to the former Maryinsky Theater. He would return to Paris in the 1920s, becoming Ida Rubinstein's collaborator in the creation of *Bolero* and other ballets.

Part 2
Modernism Comes to Ballet

THE BALLETS RUSSES' 1912 season brought the long-awaited premiere of Maurice Ravel's (1875–1937) first—and only—ballet produced by Diaghilev, *Daphnis and Chloë*, choreographed by Michel Fokine (see Garafola figs. 10, 11). It was not a happy time for Fokine, however. The more progressive members of Diaghilev's entourage, including Stravinsky, felt that the choreographer had failed to keep abreast of the modern movement.[63] Diaghilev looked instead to Vaslav Nijinsky (1890–1950), the company's star dancer, to bring a fresh artistic agenda, inviting him to make his choreographic debut with a new ballet set to Claude Debussy's (1862–1918) 1894 score, *Prélude à l'après-midi d'un faune* (*Prelude to the Afternoon of a Faun*). Diaghilev all but ignored *Daphnis*, the Ravel-Fokine ballet, giving *Faune* more rehearsal time and publicity. At the end of the 1912 Paris season, Fokine left the Ballets Russes.

Nijinsky was the first and greatest of Diaghilev's male stars, later followed by Léonide Massine, Serge Lifar, and others: young dancers to whom Diaghilev was mentor, star-maker, and lover (fig. 21). In contrast to nineteenth-century ballet tradition where the ballerina reigned supreme,

women took leading roles less frequently in the Ballets Russes. The elevation of the male body to a central role in ballet was a defining innovation of Diaghilev's enterprise, seen in many works, from *L'Après-midi d'un Faune* (1912) to *Apollon Musagète* (renamed *Apollo*, 1928). Female stars like Anna Pavlova and Ida Rubinstein saw little future with the company, and soon left to lead independent careers.

In late 1910 Nijinsky began to sketch the choreography for the new ballet, with his sister Bronislava Nijinska working closely beside him. Where Fokine had set *Firebird* and *Petrouchka* to newly composed music, Diaghilev now followed the more common practice of the time, selecting an existing score. Claude Debussy's orchestral masterpiece *Prélude à l'après-midi d'un faune* had become one of the defining works of musical modernism since its 1894 premiere. It served as a fitting vehicle for the ballet Diaghilev hoped would push the Ballets Russes beyond the innovations of Fokine's ballets.

WHEN THE FRENCH poet Stéphane Mallarmé heard Debussy's musical settings of Baudelaire's poetry around 1890, he suggested the composer adapt his poem "L'Après-midi d'un faune" (Afternoon of a Faun),[64] the dreamlike monologue of a faun—a Greek mythological figure, half human and half goat—who, after awakening from an afternoon slumber, recalls his encounters with several nymphs. Published in a famous 1876 edition with illustrations by Édouard Manet,[65] the poem became a defining expression of the French Symbolist movement. In his music, in keeping with Symbolist ideals which tended to express ideas and emotions through symbols and figurative language rather than literal representation, Debussy took an evocative approach to the scenario, later writing of his score, "Is it perhaps the dream left over at the bottom of the faun's flute?"[66]

As a student in the 1880s (fig. 22), Debussy began formulating his unique compositional voice in a series of pieces on the subject of springtime, showing an early fascination with the avant-garde innovations of Richard Wagner, and helping him to forge the musical innovations that would find their first culmination in his 1894 score, *Prélude à l'après-midi d'un faune*.[67] He played Wagner's operas at the piano and showed the German composer's musical influence in works like his 1890 settings of Baudelaire's poetry.[68] Modest Mussorgsky was another important influence; Debussy closely studied his opera *Boris Godunov*.[69]

Debussy soon moved beyond these roots, disavowing Wagner and his overpowering musical legacy that dominated European classical music at the time. While many French composers of Debussy's generation remained under the Germanic–Wagnerian spell, he found new possibilities, drawing inspiration from influences spanning Bizet to Botticelli to Japanese artists.[70] A key source of ideas was Javanese gamelan music, which he had heard at the 1889 World's Fair in Paris;[71] another was his own free experimentation—he reportedly declared around 1890 that when it comes to the creative act, "there is no theory. You have only to listen. Pleasure is the law!"[72] By 1900 Debussy had perfected an original musical language, loved for its exquisite melodies and enveloping harmonies, which would be widely admired and imitated. *Prélude à l'après-midi d'un faune* was Debussy's most-performed score during his lifetime,[73] and became a foundational work of modernism. Where Stravinsky's modernist sound would later make itself known vividly, even violently, in the pounding rhythms and wild discords of works like *The Rite of Spring*, Debussy's musical revolution was understated and subtle, yet equally profound.

↖ **Fig. 21.** Jean Cocteau (1889–1963), *Serge Diaghilev and Vaslav Nijinsky*, 1961 version of a 1913 original. The New York Public Library, Jerome Robbins Dance Division.
↑ **Fig. 22.** Marcel Baschet (1862–1941), Claude Debussy as a student, 1884. Musée d'Orsay, Paris, Gift of Marina Charrin, through the Société des Amis du Musée d'Orsay, 1996.

Debussy's Composing Score for *Prélude à l'après-midi d'un faune*

Many of the handwritten music manuscripts of Debussy, Stravinsky, and Ravel are beautiful, showing a calligraphic elegance that seems to transcend their utilitarian purpose. Debussy's 1894 manuscript for *Prélude à l'après-midi d'un faune*, here showing the famously languorous opening flute solo, is among the most important documents for the work: it is Debussy's short score (particell) from which he created the full orchestral manuscript. In just a few staves joined at the left side, he captures his ideas for the full orchestra, indicating in red and green pencil the instruments that would play each passage. He probably began composing the piece in 1891 or earlier, and completed the music in 1894, the date he inscribed on the final page of the full score manuscript.[74] This short score manuscript is notably free of revisions; Debussy preferred to work out the musical material in his head and at the piano before committing his ideas to paper,[75] though earlier sketches for the work most likely existed that are now lost.[76]

Manuscripts sometimes become meaningful artifacts in the personal lives of their creators. Debussy gave this manuscript to Gabrielle Dupont, his girlfriend between 1890 and 1898. His affectionate inscription on the first page, "To my dear and very good little Gaby, the sure affection of her devoted Claude Debussy, October 1899,"[77] was presumably a conciliatory gesture, as it was written the same month the composer married a different woman, Rosalie Texier.[78] The pianist Alfred Cortot later acquired the manuscript, adding his name. Parts of his collection were acquired by Robert Owen Lehman and are now on deposit at the Morgan Library.

Claude Debussy (1862–1918), *Prélude à l'après-midi d'un faune*, autograph manuscript, short score (particell), first and last pages (pp. 1 and 6), 1894. The Morgan Library & Museum, New York, Robert Owen Lehman Collection, on deposit.

For the ballet *L'Après-midi d'un Faune*, which Diaghilev produced in 1912 to Debussy's score, Léon Bakst (fig. 23) took a leading role in the conception. He worked closely with Diaghilev and Nijinsky in planning the work and throughout the ballet's creation, probably even suggesting details of the choreography during rehearsals, as he was known to do.[79] In keeping with Debussy's musical modernism, Bakst's costume and set designs project another, equally potent, aspect of the modernist urge: the premodern past as a source of inspiration.[80] Like many in thrall to Symbolism, including his colleagues in the World of Art, Bakst had a deep interest in ancient Greece. This fascination was evident in several of his designs for the Ballets Russes including Maurice Ravel's *Daphnis and Chloë* (1912), and for the Ida Rubinstein productions he designed such as *Hélène de Sparte* (1912; see p. 101). For *Faune*, he drew on his close study of Greek art, going back to his student days in Paris visiting the Musée du Louvre, and touring Greece in 1907 with the artist Valentin Serov (fig. 24).[81]

Bakst's vision for ballet design brought the vivid color, expressive brushwork, and other aspects of modernist painting to the theatrical domain.[82] Demonstrating his fluency with the particular demands of designing for the stage, in a 1911 interview he noted how he conceived the dancers, in the costumes he designed for them, as an integral part of his overall design idea, "like the last brushstrokes [*coups de pinceau*] of a picture . . . I reserve for the principal characters the dominant note of my canvas."[83]

The ballet's scenario, devised by Nijinsky and Bakst, takes an abstract approach that would become increasingly common in twentieth-century ballet. Rather than a story ballet with well-developed plots and characters, like *Firebird* or *Petrouchka*, *Faune* is a single short scene. Nijinsky, as the faun, reclines on a rock, watching a group of nymphs as the

↑ **Fig. 23.** Léon Bakst in Karlsbad (Karlovy Vary), 1910. Photograph by Bronislava Nijinska. Library of Congress, Bronislava Nijinska Collection.

↑   **Fig. 27.** Adolf de Meyer (1868–1946), Vaslav Nijinsky as the Faun in
L'Après-midi d'un Faune, 1912. The New York Public Library, Jerome Robbins
Dance Division.

↘   **Fig. 28.** Vaslav Nijinsky rehearsing *L'Après-midi d'un Faune* in Berlin,
December 1912. Photograph by Scherl. Nijinsky, crouching, center-left; Bronislava
Nijinska, seated at center-right in dark dress, face turned away.

tallest of them bathes (fig. 27).[84] He approaches her but she runs away, dropping her veil. He fondles it, lays it on the ground, and lowers his body over it. The Faun's final motion of the ballet, as Nijinsky's choreographic notation conveys it (see p. 72), was to relax, settling his forehead and right arm on the floor.[85] Whether or not his notation, which he created in 1915, reflects the same motions he made in the 1912 premiere, the audience interpreted that final gesture as masturbatory, provoking a contentious debate in the press which, to Diaghilev's delight, assured the ballet's fame.[86]

AS THE BALLETS Russes' newly appointed choreographer, Vaslav Nijinsky introduced a novel modernist approach to ballet composition in *Faune*. Inspired by the Greek urns he had studied at the Louvre with their processions of dancing figures,[87] he moved his dancers in two dimensions, heads and limbs twisted to the side (figs. 26–28). Where Fokine relied on pantomime and naturalistic portrayal of characters and emotions, Nijinsky's choreography turned inward, taking an analytical approach to the workings and mechanics of the individual body, and exploring geometric conceptions of space that opened the possibility to express abstract symbolic meaning through dance.[88] His dancers rebelled at the difficult poses and movements which asked of them a severe degree of exactitude. As Bronislava Nijinska recalled, "In all of Nijinsky's ballets, the . . . body position of each separate dancer was precisely defined and brought . . . to the precise position for every finger on the hand," an approach "not customary for the corps-de-ballet" and which provoked "protests on the part of the exhausted dancers [that] required intervention from Diaghilev himself, primarily to calm Nijinsky."[89]

At the premiere, Claude Debussy was horrified, finding an "appalling dissonance" between his music and Nijinsky's choreography.[90] Nijinsky himself noted that his choreography did not adhere tightly to the music, working instead in tension or counterpoint with it. Others felt that the music even became an accompanying element to Nijinsky's striking dance design. However, close analysis reveals a precise, if free, connection between music and dance.[91]

Diaghilev continued to program *L'Après-midi d'un Faune* throughout the Ballets Russes' existence. The ballet came to define an era in choreography and established a new independence for the art form. With just four ballets to his name,[92] Nijinsky is regarded as a revolutionary choreographer. Igor Markevich, a composer who worked with Diaghilev in the late 1920s, wrote in 1978, "If Nijinsky the dancer represented the supreme culmination of centuries of aesthetic progress, especially in classical dance, Nijinsky the choreographer, that is to say the creator in him, appears with the hindsight of time as one of the boldest revolutionaries in the history of Art. With him modern dance begins."[93]

Nijinsky's Notations for *L'Après-midi d'un Faune*

In 1913, the year after the first performance of *L'Après-midi d'un Faune*, Vaslav Nijinsky wrote down some of his choreographic ideas for the ballet.[94] He used a dance notation of his own invention which he adapted from Stepanov notation, a system he had studied in the curriculum of the Imperial Ballet School. Both Stepanov's and Nijinsky's systems use a modified form of music notation.[95] While duration signs (quarter notes, half notes, rests, and so forth) retain similar meaning, indicating the timing of the dancer's movements (ties for pauses, rests for dancers' exit points), other elements take on new meaning: three staves, joined at the left side, indicate three areas of the body—head/torso (top staff), arms (middle), and legs (lower). Notes on the staff, rather than indicating pitch (how high or low a note is), show the direction and level of the moving parts of the body.[96]

In 1915 Nijinsky pursued his notation project further, creating a complete dance score for *L'Après-midi d'un Faune*. His notation system, now more fully developed, was among the first to describe every part of the body, showing precise postures which, when performed in succession, yield continuous movement.[97] His system, which he would elaborate and refine in a series of notebooks from 1917 to 1919 (see pp. 78–79), bore the potential to serve as a prescriptive blueprint from which dancers could reproduce movement, from the notation alone, to create a new performance—much as music notation allows a composer to communicate any combination of pitches and rhythms for the performer to play without having heard the music before

(at least as an ideal: music notation cannot capture every aspect of performance).

Dance scholar Claudia Jeschke notes how Nijinsky's method of communicating bodily motion through a notation system "opens up the potential for a new, abstract movement repertoire."[98] On the written page, "the body itself becomes a precisely configurable space for movement, a stage."[99] His innovations are both reflected in, and enabled by, his use of notation.

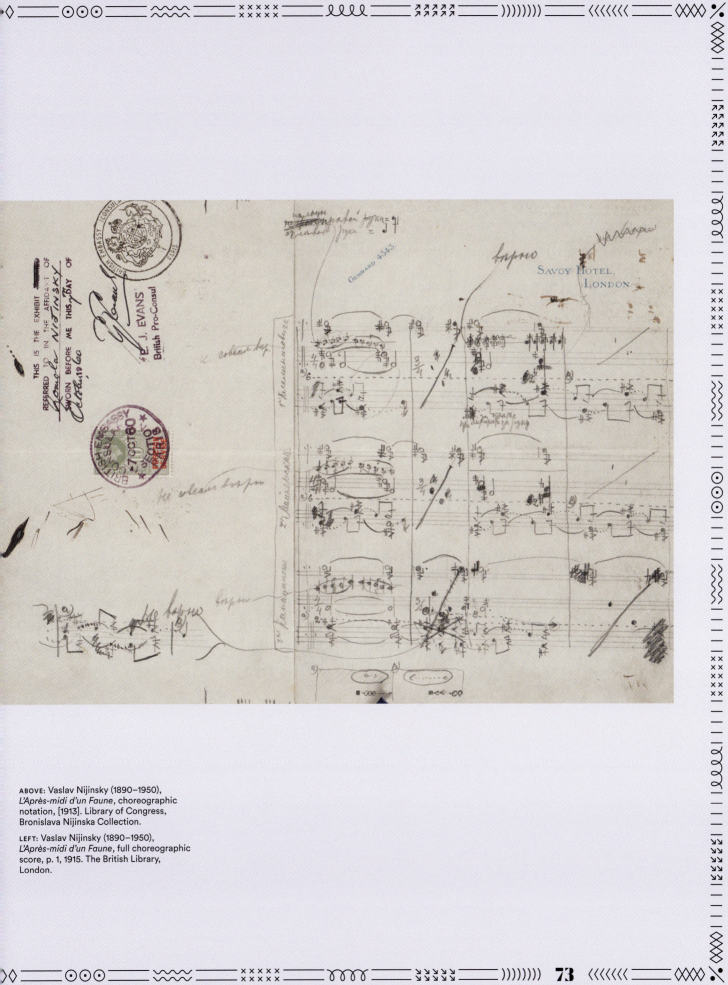

ABOVE: Vaslav Nijinsky (1890–1950),
L'Après-midi d'un Faune, choreographic
notation, [1913]. Library of Congress,
Bronislava Nijinska Collection.

LEFT: Vaslav Nijinsky (1890–1950),
L'Après-midi d'un Faune, full choreographic
score, p. 1, 1915. The British Library,
London.

Mlle NIJINSKA, dans *Petrouchka*.

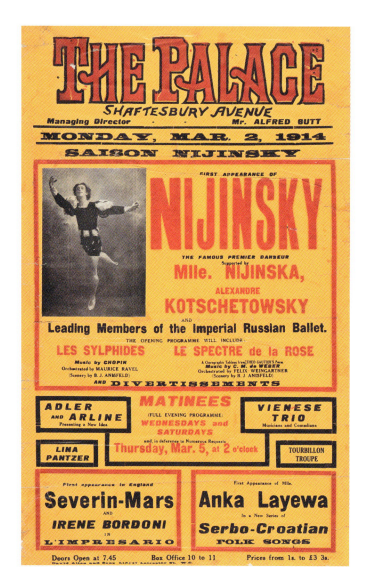

NIJINSKY DID NOT accomplish his innovations alone. As he choreographed *L'Après-midi d'un Faune*, his younger sister, Bronislava Nijinska (1891–1972), was his confidante and creative partner. Brother and sister played Debussy's score for each other at the piano, with Nijinsky molding the choreography on his sister's body. She danced in the ballet's 1912 premiere as one of the nymphs (see fig. 26).

Like her brother, Bronislava Nijinska had studied at the Imperial Ballet School in St. Petersburg, and like him she came to Paris in 1909 with Diaghilev's troupe—he as a star dancer and she as a member of the corps de ballet. She appeared as one of the princesses in *Firebird* in 1910,[100] and danced one of her first solo roles in *Petrouchka* (fig. 29). Critics praised her skill as a dancer, including Stravinsky who called her "extremely talented . . . fully the equal of her brother."[101]

Nijinsky's and Nijinska's relationship is a moving study in friendship, the ties of siblings, and creative partnership. He was famous from a young age; she lived and danced in his shadow. Although she was devoted to her brother, her memoirs, written years later, reveal the tensions in their relationship.[102] For the 1913 season he gave her lead roles in *Jeux* and in *The Rite of Spring*, and, as she had done with *Faune*, she worked closely with him on both ballets, imagining and trying out the choreography.[103] But when he learned that Nijinska was pregnant with her first child, Nijinsky dropped her from both productions.[104] Yet Nijinska remained loyal to her brother, once even quitting her coveted position at the Maryinsky Theater in protest when the director fired him for wearing an improper outfit in 1911. During a tour to South America in September 1913, Nijinsky married Romola de Pulszky, a fellow dancer, ending his romantic relationship with Diaghilev. Enraged, the impresario fired Nijinsky. Once more Nijinska stayed by his side, leaving the Ballets Russes.

The two formed a new ballet company for a 1914 Saison Nijinsky at London's Palace Theatre (fig. 30). Nijinska did a little of everything, hiring the dancers, leading rehearsals as ballet master, and taking over Tamara Karsavina's role as Nijinsky's dance partner on stage. Among other projects, they approached Maurice Ravel to orchestrate Chopin's music for

←← **Fig. 29.** Bronislava Nijinska (1891–1972) as the Street Dancer in *Petrouchka*, 1911. Reproduced in program for Diaghilev's eighth season in Paris, 21 June 1913. The Morgan Library & Museum, New York, James Fuld Collection.
← **Fig. 30.** Poster for 1914 Saison Nijinsky, London, "The famous premier danseur / supported by Mlle. Nijinska." Library of Congress, Bronislava Nijinska Collection.
↓ **Fig. 31.** Maurice Ravel (left), with Vaslav Nijinsky and Bronislava Nijinska in Paris, 1914.

Nijinsky's revised version of Fokine's Ballets Russes classic, *Les Sylphides* (fig. 31). When Nijinsky fell ill after only three weeks of performances, Saison Nijinsky ended its short run. As World War I began in summer 1914, brother and sister went separate ways, he to Vienna with his wife, and she to St. Petersburg with her husband.[105] They would not see each other again until 1921, when Nijinska returned to Western Europe to find her brother in the grips of the mental illness that would permanently remove him from public life.

In 1917–19, the last years before his hospitalization, Nijinsky created a haunting series of drawings. Many appear to depict the human eye; deeply affected by the war, Nijinsky reportedly said that they were the faces of soldiers.[106] Several of his 1919 drawings were used to illustrate the first 1936 and 1937 editions of his *Diary* (fig. 32).[107] In the circles that dominate his dance notations of the same period (see p. 79), there is continuity with his artwork, full of circles and curves (fig. 33).

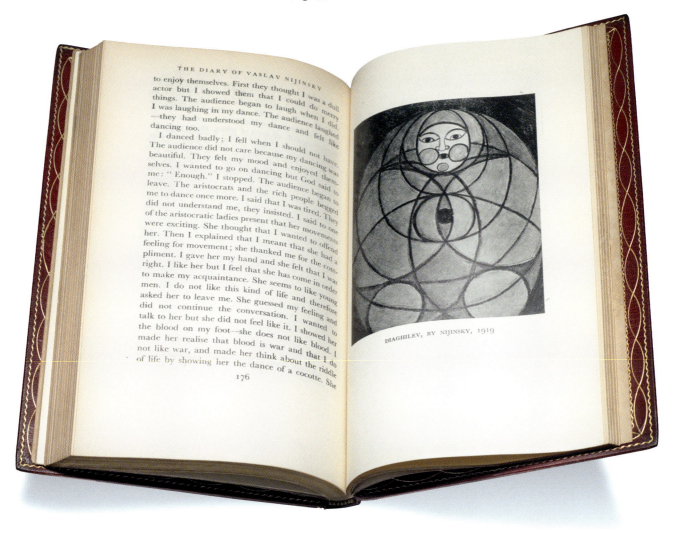

DIAGHILEV, BY NIJINSKY, 1919

← **Fig. 32.** Vaslav Nijinsky (1890–1950), *Diary*, p. 176 and facing plate (London: Victor Gollancz, 1937). The Morgan Library & Museum, Mary Flagler Cary Music Collection, purchased 2022. Reproduction of Nijinsky's portrait of Serge Diaghilev, 1919.
↑ **Fig. 33.** Vaslav Nijinsky (1890–1950), *Dancer*, 1917–18. John Neumeier Foundation, Hamburg.

Nijinsky's Dance Notation, 1917–1919

This notebook is the last in a series Vaslav Nijinsky used between 1917 and 1919. In pencil, he continues the dance notation project he had begun in 1913 with *L'Après-midi d'un Faune* based on the Stepanov notation system (see pp. 72–73). Then, beginning from the back of the notebook, upside down in black pen, he takes up the literary work which would become famous as "Nijinsky's Diary" following its first publication in 1936.[108]

In these later notation notebooks of 1917–19, Nijinsky modifies the elements of traditional music notation further than he had done in his 1915 score for *L'Après-midi d'un Faune*. Using a three-line staff rather than five lines as before, he distills movement to its essential elements, founding it in principles of the circle (circular diagrams appear throughout the notebooks).[109]

In these notebooks Nijinsky sought a comprehensive system for dance notation. He titled one notebook "Theory of writing down all human movements and poses according to the system."[110] In a 1916 interview, he made clear his ambitions: "This book is to be my real life work. . . . The idea is to write down the dance even as music is recorded through the medium of notation and literary ideas through the written word. I claim no priority . . . for a century or more, projects tending to this end have claimed the attention of authorities. . . . The collapse of innumerable experiments has been due only to the persistent failure to discover a comprehensive system of communicating terpsichorean [dance] ideas. Too much complication and too little directness defeated the professed aims. Well, I have overcome that obstacle."[111]

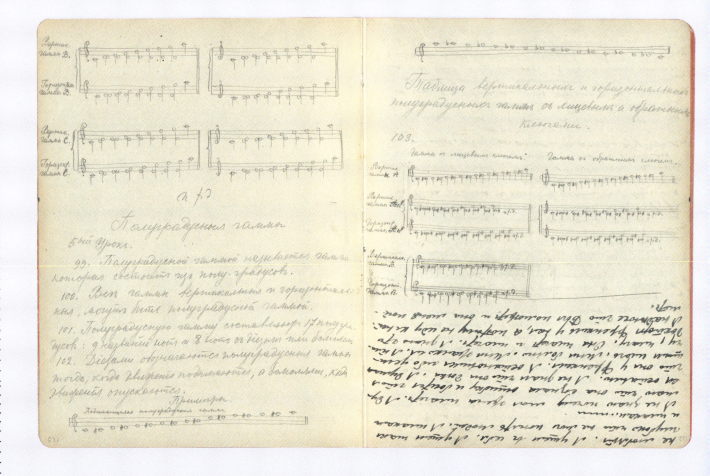

Nijinsky seems to have intended to do for the art of dance what Guido of Arezzo, the tenth-century monk credited with inventing the system of staff lines and notes still used today, had done for music: to create the basis for a written tradition that could be widely adopted and, over time, build a repertory of dance scores and known, repeatable dance works. Wendy Lesser expresses the problem Nijinsky was addressing: "Dance is our most ephemeral art. By comparison, literature, painting and sculpture are practically eternal. Even music and theater,

though they too exist in the moment, can be written down and effectively reconstructed.... Dance notation has proved woefully inadequate,[112] and even preservatives like film and videotape do not eliminate the need for personal instruction, because the camera isn't always looking where you want it to."[113]

Nijinsky's ambitions for his dance notation never came to fruition. Partly because his project coincided with the onset of his mental illness, and despite—or perhaps abetted by—his legendary status as a dancer, his work

as a notator was not taken seriously during his lifetime and remained little noticed or understood until the 1970s, when his notebooks first became accessible to scholars. In the 1980s, Ann Hutchinson Guest and Claudia Jeschke deciphered his 1915 score for *Faune* for the first time (see p. 72) and began to decode the notation system he developed between 1917 and 1919.[114]

Vaslav Nijinsky (1890–1950), Notebook containing dance notation (pencil) and drafts for the *Diary* (pen), pp. 122–23, 134–35, 1918–19. The New York Public Library, Jerome Robbins Dance Division.

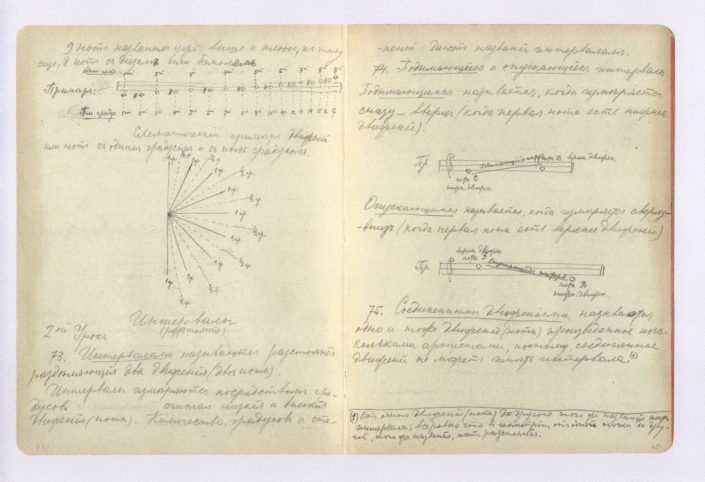

Bronislava Nijinska returned to St. Petersburg in 1914, where she choreographed her first dances.[115] The following year she moved to Kyiv, where she performed at the city's opera theater and in 1919 founded the School of Movement, just as the Bolsheviks took over the city and only weeks after the birth of her son. Allying herself with the new Soviet arts bureaucracy, she choreographed her first modern works and created her first performing ensemble. "The main goal of the school," she wrote, "is to create an entirely new breed of dancer . . . for whom art is an essential need and an expansion of their spiritual state. . . . My school is the program of my life."[116]

It was here in Kyiv, cut off from her brother, from Diaghilev, and from the world of ballet that had nurtured her in St. Petersburg and Paris, that Nijinska came into her own as a choreographer. She created her first plotless ballets, honing the idea that classical ballet techniques did not need to be rejected, as Isadora Duncan and other "free dancers" of the period had done, but could be repurposed through a new, modernist aesthetic.[117] Echoing her brother's approach in *L'Après-midi d'un Faune* (see p. 71), Nijinska recognized that choreography could have a presence within a work that was partly independent of the musical score—a theme that would be borne out in the ballets she would produce with Diaghilev and Rubinstein in the 1920s including *Les Noces*, *Les Biches*, and *Bolero*. Taking this freedom from music a step further, she choreographed a silent ballet, *Fear*, for which her colleague in Kyiv, Vadym Meller, made a striking costume illustration evoking Nijinska in the act of dancing (fig. 34). Like the costume illustrations of Léon Bakst (see figs. 13, 14, 20, 25), Meller's drawing captures an idea, an effect, rather than serving as a precise blueprint for a costume.

Nijinska looked to visual art as a conceptual analogue for her new dance creations, finding resonance with her ideas in contemporary abstract painting. "Pictorial art," she wrote, "must cast aside the naturalism that enchains it. . . . I want to approach a picture and see only a symphony of colors."[118] Nijinska's own drawings of the period show her interest in spatiality and circles as principles for bodily movement, referencing Constructivist methods and recalling her brother's circle-based designs in his notebooks of the same period (see pp. 78–79)—a synergy particularly notable since the siblings had almost no contact with each other during this period.[119] In a series of striking geometric choreographic drawings Nijinska made in 1919 in Kyiv, she notes, for example beneath the panel at lower right, "Combinations: Circular movements" (fig. 35).[120]

↑   **Fig. 34.** Vadym Meller (1884–1962), Costume illustration for Bronislava Nijinska in *Fear*, Kyiv, 1919. Library of Congress, Bronislava Nijinska Collection.
→   **Fig. 35.** Bronislava Nijinska (1891–1972), Choreographic drawings, Kyiv, 1919. Library of Congress, Bronislava Nijinska Collection.

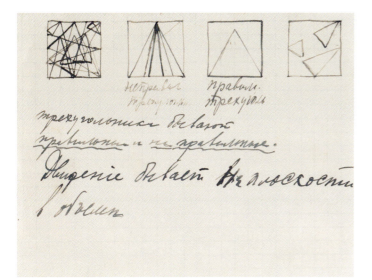

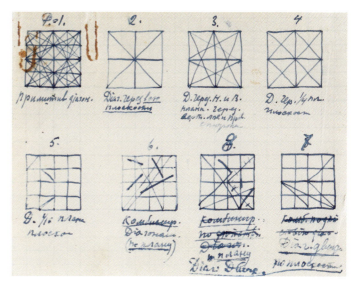

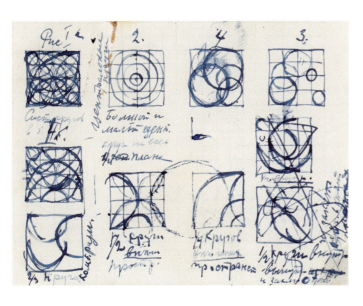

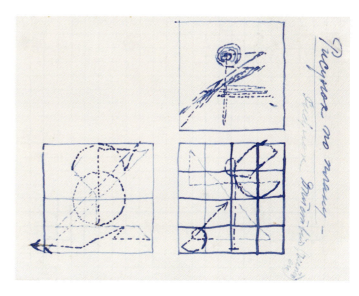

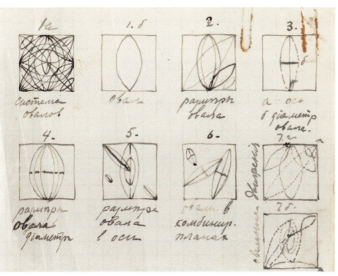

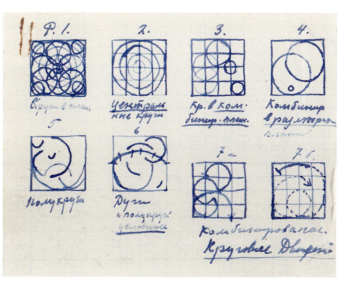

↑   **Fig. 36.** Bronislava Nijinska (1891–1972), Self-portrait, 1921.
Library of Congress, Bronislava Nijinska Collection.
→   **Fig. 37.** Bronislava Nijinska in 1921 after leaving Kyiv.
Library of Congress, Bronislava Nijinska Collection.

In April 1920, when she learned of her brother's deteriorating mental health, she was devastated. After hesitating, unprepared to abandon her school and performing group in Kyiv,[121] finally in March 1921, at great risk, she smuggled herself and her family over the border. Her diary entry for 2 June 1921, is stark. "I'm in Vienna. Vatsa [Nijinsky] is very ill. . . . He recognizes neither me nor our mother. . . . He lost himself in his visions and forgot the way back. I will finish all his work and expand whatever I can. I will return to 'my own' work as the continuation of Vaslav's art. . . . Now there will be more, and it will be better."[122] On the back of a self-portrait she drew shortly after returning to Western Europe, she wrote, "I'll bury myself into [work] so as not to fear my own life and pain, to obliterate everything. [I wish] God [would help] me to go to Sergei Pavlovich [Diaghilev]. My yearning for truth would create the Big Truth [in ballet?]" (fig. 36).[123]

Just in time, Serge Diaghilev—always one to connect creative souls with their destiny—invited Nijinska to dance again for the Ballets Russes,[124] and to choreograph for him for the first time. Her initial project was to rechoreograph a number of dances for Diaghilev's lavish revival of Tchaikovsky's *The Sleeping Beauty* (retitled *The Sleeping Princess*) (see Garafola fig. 19). On the strength of her work, Diaghilev hired her as the first and only female choreographer of the Ballets Russes (fig. 38). Her first full project was to stage Stravinsky's ballet about a fox, *Le Renard*, for the 1922 season (see Garafola figs. 20, 21).[125] Her next project would be her masterpiece: *Les Noces*, with music by Stravinsky, premiered in 1923.

IGOR STRAVINSKY HAD first conceived *Les Noces* in 1912, intending it as his next great Russian ballet to follow *Firebird*, *Petrouchka*, and *The Rite of Spring*. As with the others, he turned to Russian culture, this time a traditional peasant wedding. Like the *Rite*, the subject of the new work would be a solemn ritual centered around a young woman, a "depiction of a sacrament . . . a work of dignity and reserve, and finally of exaltation."[126] A passage from Alexander Pushkin's 1833 novel *Eugene Onegin*, that many Russians of Stravinsky's generation knew by heart captures the experience of the bride at the center of the story. A nurse recalls her wedding:

> . . . a woman matchmaker kept visiting
> my kinsfolk, and at last
> my father blessed me. Bitterly
> I cried for fear; and, crying
> they unbraided my tress and, chanting
> they led me to the church.
> And so I entered a strange family. . . [127]

Drawing from wedding songs he found in popular Russian literature and song compilations, Stravinsky created a text for the sung parts, rich in prayer and folklore, evoking the rigid wedding rituals.[128] The scenario in four tableaus is simple. Two plots proceed in parallel, the Bride's

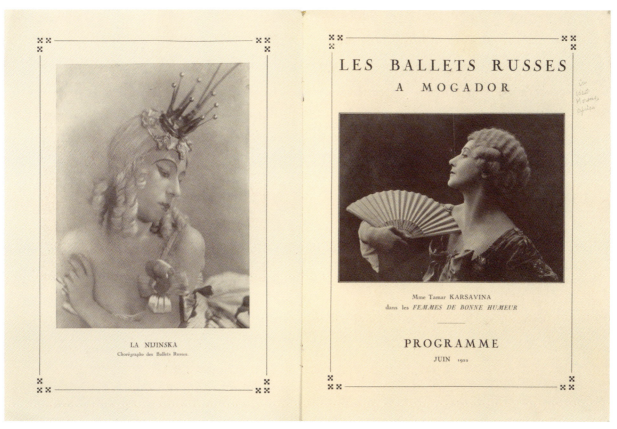

↑   **Fig. 38.** "Les Ballets Russes à Mogador" program, [Paris], June 1922. The Morgan Library & Museum, James Fuld Collection.

↑ ↗ **Fig. 39.** Igor Stravinsky (1882–1971), *Les Noces*, autograph manuscript, first draft in short score (particell) of the first tableau (to rehearsal [16] in the published score), versions 1–3, [1914–15]. Vellum cover hand-painted by Stravinsky. The Morgan Library & Museum, New York, Robert Owen Lehman Collection, on deposit.

→→ **Fig. 40.** Pablo Picasso (1881–1973), *Portrait of Igor Stravinsky*, Rome, 1917. Private collection.

preparations and the Groom's, with a touching farewell between the Bride and her mother. The two stories merge in the final tableau, "The Wedding Feast," at the end of which the couple disappears into the bedchamber.

Stravinsky took three years to finish *Les Noces* and another five experimenting with different ways to orchestrate it, producing over a thousand pages of drafts and sketches. A manuscript in the Robert Owen Lehman Collection, Stravinsky's first short-score (particell) draft created in 1914–15, provides key evidence for the early stages of his compositional process (fig. 39). When he met Diaghilev in February 1915 in Rome, Stravinsky may have already drafted much of the first tableau, as shown in this sketch. Like *The Rite of Spring*, *Les Noces* is a deeply Russian work, reflected in the beautiful design Stravinsky painted on the cover of this manuscript, in a Neo-Primitivist folkloric style, with the Russian title of the ballet, "Svadebka." Early sketches show that he originally intended a massive orchestra for *Les Noces*, like that of *The Rite of Spring* (which he had completed not long before), or even two orchestras together, requiring over 150 musicians.

Diaghilev fell in love with the music of *Les Noces* and was eager for the score to be completed quickly.[129] The premiere was announced for the following season, 1916.[130] But because of the war, the Russian Revolution, and other disruptions, the work was postponed again and again. Moreover, Stravinsky was not finished experimenting. A 1919 version with pianola (see p. 87), a mechanical piano, reflected his fascination with new technologies of the time including radio and phonographs.[131] Responding to new aesthetics of Mechanism and Cubism, as well as the stirrings of neo-classicism, Stravinsky reworked the instrumentation again for a mixture of cimbaloms, harmonium, pianola, and percussion.[132] When that version was not practical for performance, he revised it yet again, completing the final score only a few weeks before the June 1923 premiere. *Les Noces*, as audiences have known the music ever since, is a spare combination of four pianos, percussion ensemble, choir, and vocal soloists—a sound the composer described as "perfectly homogeneous, perfectly impersonal, and perfectly mechanical."[133] Its percussion-dominated instrumentation, unusual at the time, would be widely imitated and adapted by composers in the twentieth century.

Stravinsky Composes *Les Noces*, 1914–1919

Stravinsky's early ideas for *Les Noces* are reflected in this 1914–15 manuscript of his first full orchestra sketches for the ballet (also see fig. 39). In works of the same period like *Podblyudniye: Four Russian Peasant Songs* (1917), which served as a study for *Les Noces*, Stravinsky researched folk song sources, as he had done for *Petrouchka* and other works, finding new ways to integrate them into a fresh, modernist style.[134]

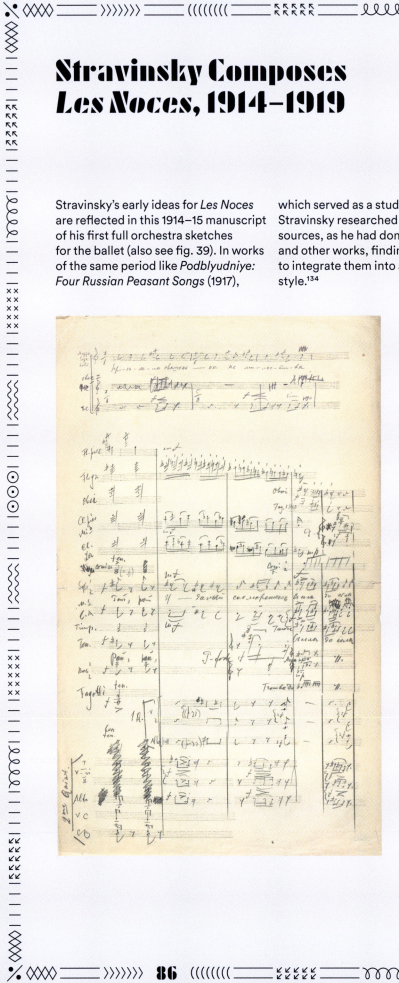

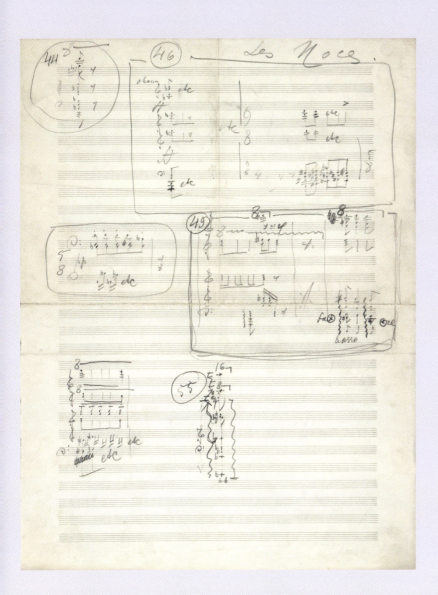

In 1919 the composer sketched a version of *Les Noces* that included pianola, the mechanized playerless piano popular at the time.[135] From around 1914 Stravinsky had been interested in the instrument, seeking ways to exert more control over the sound of his music, particularly rhythm.[136] He contracted with the Pleyel Company to create a series of illustrated piano rolls for *Firebird*, *Petrouchka*, and *The Rite of Spring*.[137] Dancers recall a pianola recording being used during rehearsals for *Les Noces*.[138] It is likely Stravinsky requested it, wanting assurance of the consistency of the tempo, though this proved elusive due to limitations of the technology.

LEFT: Igor Stravinsky (1882–1971), *Les Noces*, autograph manuscript, full-score sketches for the third tableau, [1914–15]. The Morgan Library & Museum, Robert Owen Lehman Collection, on deposit.

ABOVE: Igor Stravinsky (1882–1971), *Les Noces*, autograph manuscript, drafts for pianola arrangement, ca. 1919. The Morgan Library & Museum, New York, Mary Flagler Cary Music Collection, purchased with the special assistance of the Ann and Gordon Getty Foundation.

RIGHT: Igor Stravinsky at the pianola, August 1923. Photograph by Vera Sudeikina (1889–1982). Paul Sacher Stiftung, Sammlung Igor Stravinsky, Basel.

FOR *LES NOCES*'s designs Diaghilev turned to Natalia Goncharova (1881–1962), one of the outstanding avant-garde Russian artists of the twentieth century. Her vivid Neo-Primitivist evocations of Russian folk art, whose "bright colors, crude forms, 'wrong proportions,' and a wonderful joviality and optimism"[139] informed by her deep study of Russian handcrafts and rituals, had been showcased in the Ballets Russes' 1914 production of Nikolai Rimsky-Korsakov's opera *Le Coq d'Or*. With her partner (in life and in art) Mikhail Larionov, she had entered Diaghilev's circle on the eve of World War I, replacing Bakst and Benois. In Goncharova's work Diaghilev saw the perfect match for Stravinsky's new ballet, and she set to work on *Les Noces* in 1915.[140]

Like Stravinsky, Goncharova took her concept for the ballet through several stages, from her brightly colored drawings of 1915 (fig. 41) to a set of designs in 1921 in cooler colors.[141] When Bronislava Nijinska saw the designs in 1922, however, they did not suit her idea of Stravinsky's score. As she later wrote, "to interpret the libretto as the merrymaking of Russian peasants against a pictorial background of sheer exuberance and unalloyed joy would serve to defeat the inherent tragedy."[142] When Nijinska shared her objections with Diaghilev, he dropped her from the project. But when he returned to *Les Noces* in 1923, he agreed to stage the ballet as Nijinska intended it, and she rejoined. After Goncharova sat in on rehearsals and discussed the choreography with Nijinska, she understood the choreographer's vision for the ballet, and created the stark visual concept seen in her final stage and costume designs (figs. 43, 44),[143] even modeling some drawings after Nijinska's choreographic formations (figs. 44, 45).

↑   **Fig. 41.** Natalia Goncharova (1881–1962), Curtain design for *Les Noces*, 1915. Philadelphia Museum of Art. Two firebirds of Russian folk legend escort the couple, bride on the left, groom on the right.

←   **Fig. 42.** Natalia Goncharova (1881–1962), *Self-Portrait*, ca. 1907. Mead Art Museum, Amherst College, gift of Thomas P. Whitney.

↑ **Fig. 43.** Natalia Goncharova (1881–1962), Sketch for the stage design for *Les Noces*, 1923. The New York Public Library, Jerome Robbins Dance Division.

Working with Stravinsky in the final weeks before the June 1923 premiere, Nijinska took in stride his desire for control. In one letter he wrote to her, "Dear Bronya, Sergei [Diaghilev] said to me that you and him are not clear on the reprise at the beginning of [*Les Noces*]. Now listen carefully! At the lower end of the first page under No. 1, where it says 'curtain,' the music is [musical notation] . . . ending [musical notation]" (fig. 46).[144] Although the ballet came together through a collaborative process between composer, choreographer, and designer, Nijinska's creative influence was crucial. She later wrote, "*Les Noces* was the only ballet in which [Diaghilev] allowed the choreographer a deciding influence over the entire production."[145] The combined effect of music, choreography, and design represented a culmination of the artistic vision she had developed during her time in Kyiv. She embraced abstraction, in keeping with the broader trends toward abstract art during that era, overcoming Diaghilev's objections. "In my theatre of 1920 [in Kyiv] my first works . . . were . . . ballets 'without libretti.' Diaghileff did not sympathise with the idea. . . . [I]n spite of this, with great efforts, I was able to carry my ideas . . . into my productions with Diaghileff. . . . *Noces* was the first work where the libretto was a hidden theme for a pure choreography; it was a choreographic con-

certo."[146] In her choreography for *Les Noces*, Nijinska revitalized classical ballet methods to fresh effect, drawing on folk dance—reflecting Stravinsky's and Goncharova's own references to folk traditions in the ballet—and unique methods she developed, for example using pointework, a classical technique, to evoke key symbols in the ballet such as the braiding of the Bride's hair[147] and sexual penetration.[148]

At the June 1923 premiere of *Les Noces* in Paris, critics were impressed.[149] The ballet is considered Nijinska's masterpiece. While *The Rite of Spring* is Stravinsky's most famous ballet, *Les Noces* is one of his most admired and influential scores, and despite his mechanistic conception, it is among his most emotionally powerful dance works. Diaghilev, who had a special affection for the work, and to whom Stravinsky dedicated the score, wrote:

> In the modern epoch of Russian music, and perhaps of the music of the world, there have been two masterpieces produced on the stage: [Mussorgsky's] *Boris Godunov* and *Noces*. . . . If you wish to know an essentially Russian work, to my mind nothing reveals Russia as completely as does *Noces* . . . this work contains the essence itself of the Russian soil. . . .[150]

↑↑ **Fig. 44.** Natalia Goncharova (1881–1962), Drawing of women in Nijinska's choreographic braid motif for *Les Noces*, 1923. Harvard Theatre Collection, Houghton Library, Howard D. Rothschild Collection.
↑ **Fig. 45.** Dancers on stage in *Les Noces*, 1923. Library of Congress, Bronislava Nijinska Collection.

↑ **Fig. 46.** Igor Stravinsky (1882–1971), Letter to Bronislava Nijinska regarding *Les Noces*, 27 March 1923. Library of Congress, Bronislava Nijinska Collection.

In 1924 Nijinska followed her triumph in *Les Noces* with another masterpiece for the Ballets Russes, *Les Biches* (Garafola fig. 22), with music by the French composer Francis Poulenc and designs by French artist Marie Laurencin. The ballet carried forward ideas Nijinska had developed with her brother a decade before in *Jeux* (1913) (see Garafola fig. 9), updated with the chic modernism of the 1920s. After three more ballets for Diaghilev, Nijinska's relationship with the impresario and his all-male inner circle became increasingly rocky.[151] Once more, she moved on, joining all those—Benois, Bakst, Rubinstein, Fokine, Nijinsky—whose careers Diaghilev had made possible, yet whose tenure with the Ballets Russes had been intense but brief. While many women choreographed ballets during the era, few worked for prestigious institutions or were credited as authors of lasting dance works. Nijinska's time as choreographer of the Ballets Russes provided a platform for the world to recognize the value of her work and secured her a place in the modernist tradition.[152]

In 1925 Nijinska founded her own ballet company, the Theatre Choréographique Nijinska [*sic*], choreographing another Stravinsky score, *Ragtime*.[153] In 1926 and 1927 she choreographed two seasons at the Teatro Colón in Buenos Aires, spending long periods away from her family. By 1928 she was ready, and eager, to accept an invitation from Ida Rubinstein, the Paris theater celebrity and early star of the Ballets Russes, to choreograph for her new ballet company, Les Ballets de Madame Ida Rubinstein.

Nijinska's Diverse Notation Strategies for *Les Noces*

"You listen to music through your ears— yes? I listen to music through my eyes. I want my ballets to be music through the eyes, so if you would close your ears you could still hear the music—you could see the music. A paradox! But a paradox close to the center of my idea of ballet."
—Bronislava Nijinska[154]

Bronislava Nijinska showed her concern for the preservation of the modernist choreographic tradition her brother had pursued in *Faune* and *The Rite of Spring*, which she carried forward in *Les Noces* and other works. In 1924 she wrote, "When . . . the masterpieces of choreographic composition disappear with their creator, how to save everything that has been done in our time? . . . We have nothing real except legends of remarkable male and female dancers; no recorded scores of compositions."[155] Nijinska saw the solution not in developing a comprehensive system of dance notation, as her brother had sought to do, but in the founding of a ballet "conservatory" like the one she had created in Kyiv. Like most

choreographers, her primary creation took place in person, working directly with dancers.

Yet Nijinska's engagement with the written page was intense and extensive, and her dance notation reveals much about her choreographic ideas. Her large archive at the Library of Congress preserves her diverse approaches to conceiving and communicating dance on paper, including hundreds of pages of drawings, geometric designs, numbering systems, floor patterns, music notation, and annotated musi-

cal scores, showing her skills as artist, musician, and dancer.[156]

Nijinska drew upon a broad repertory of notational strategies. Claudia Jeschke notes how Nijinska "emphasize[s] dynamic or plastic concentrations, climaxes, essential aspects of the choreography through more pressure on the pen, through broader or darker strokes. . ." suggesting "the immediate (self-embodied, self-experienced) movements of an active dancer," and a focus on the audience's viewpoint.[157] In a set of 1923 elevation views for *Les Noces*, showing specific body positions and group formations, she describes for example her drawing in the lower right corner: "another grouping is in profile, they are stretched out on top of each other"—one of the ballet's iconic formations at the end of the first tableau and the opening of the third, at the Bride's home.[158]

ABOVE: Bronislava Nijinska, at center, rehearsing *Les Noces* in Monte Carlo, 1923. Library of Congress, Bronislava Nijinska Collection.

LEFT: Bronislava Nijinska (1891–1972), Choreographic drawings for *Les Noces*: frontal elevation views of dancers for the first tableau, 1923. Library of Congress, Bronislava Nijinska Collection.

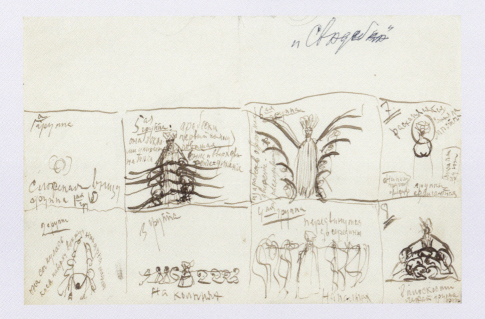

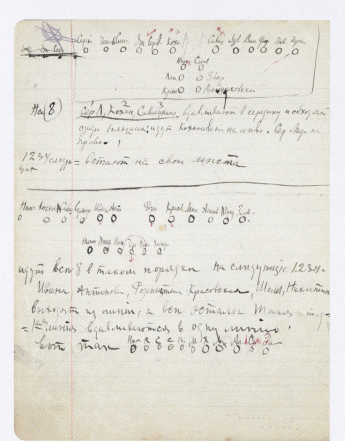

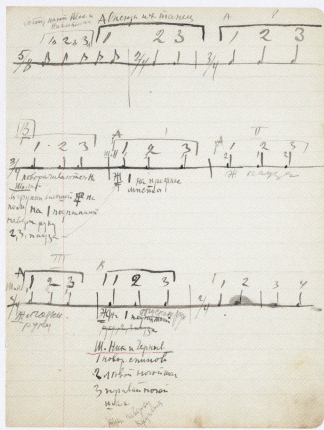

Nijinska also employed plan views of the stage seen from above, like those of Michel Fokine for *Firebird* (see p. 56), indicating the position of each dancer as a small empty or filled circle.[159] One notebook lists by name the performers who appeared in the premiere (leaf 6v). In a following sketch (leaf 8), which shows the ballet's fourth and final scene, she draws upon her fluency with music notation. Using brackets above the staff, she marks what she called "choreographic measures, which correspond neither to the rhythm of the musical measures nor to the sonority of the music"[160]—in this case 3/4 time (three beats per measure) overlaid on Stravinsky's musical measures of 5/8, 2/4, and 3/4 time.[161]

Like Nijinsky and Fokine, Nijinska was musically skilled, reading scores fluently. Her heavily annotated score for *Les Noces* includes her verbal instructions, drawings of dance positions, and brackets above the staff indicating her "choreographic measures" (also seen in the previous image). Her inscriptions in pen in the middle of page 5, typical of those throughout the score, begin: "with the right leg below on the arm[;] the second arm reunites with the first arm."[162] As a student at the Imperial Ballet School, Nijinska, like her brother, mastered Stepanov dance notation, a system of precise bodily movements based on music notation (see p. 73)[163] and occasionally adapted Stepanov elements, as in her notations for *Le Baiser de la Fée* (*The Fairy's Kiss*), the 1928 Stravinsky ballet for Ida Rubinstein.[164]

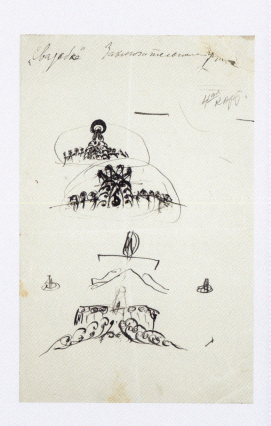

LEFT: Bronislava Nijinska (1891–1972), Choreographic notes for the fourth tableau of *Les Noces*, 1923. Library of Congress, Bronislava Nijinska Collection. On left: Floor plans with locations and names of dancers who appeared in the first performance; right: Choreographic rhythms in brackets.

RIGHT: Igor Stravinsky (1882–1971), *Les Noces*, piano-vocal score with choreographic annotations by Bronislava Nijinska (1891–1972) for the first tableau, p. 5, 1923. Library of Congress, Bronislava Nijinska Collection.

BELOW LEFT: Bronislava Nijinska (1891–1972), Choreographic drawings for *Les Noces*: frontal elevation views of dancers for the fourth tableau, ca. 1923. Library of Congress, Bronislava Nijinska Collection.

BELOW: Bronislava Nijinska rehearsing the fourth tableau of *Les Noces* for the 1966 Royal Ballet production. Library of Congress, Bronislava Nijinska Collection.

A photograph shows Nijinska rehearsing her 1966 revival of *Les Noces* at the Royal Ballet. The group formation matches the one seen in the drawing she made for the same moment in the original 1923 production, which she labeled "The final grouping [pencil:] the 4th tableau"—showing one of the ballet's most memorable moments, as the lights go down after the couple retreats to the bedchamber.

Part 3
A New Fusion:
Neo-Romanticism and
the Twentieth Century

IDA RUBINSTEIN, a star of Diaghilev's first two seasons in Paris, had left the Ballets Russes to pursue her career independently, producing a series of stage works through the 1910s and 1920s. In 1928, she founded a new ballet company that would briefly rival the Ballets Russes.

Born in Ukraine to a wealthy family, Ida Rubinstein was raised in luxurious and cultivated surroundings in St. Petersburg. From her teens she devoted her life to the stage, drawn to what she saw as the transformative power of art. In 1904, barely twenty-one, she buttonholed the artist Léon Bakst, and as a young woman with no professional performing experience, convinced him to design a production of Sophocles's *Antigone* around her.[165] For 1908 she planned a performance of Oscar Wilde's play *Salomé*, engaging Bakst again, and the choreographer Michel Fokine as her dance teacher.[166] The St. Petersburg authorities canceled Wilde's play, which they considered scandalous. But in a ploy devised with Bakst, Rubinstein thwarted the censor by performing it without words, miming the entire drama. "To understand the audacity of this project," Bakst recalled, "consider the state of society in St. Petersburg at the time: very orthodox, hypocritically prudish, and strictly subject to the decisions of the Holy Synod."[167]

It was probably that same evening that Serge Diaghilev, in the audience for *Salomé*, decided to feature Rubinstein in his first Paris ballet season the following June. She appeared as Cleopatra in 1909 and the next year as Zobéide, the unfaithful queen murdered by her husband in *Schéhérazade*. Alexandre Benois recalled how a "big trump card in our Paris success was the appearance of Ida Rubinstein."[168] She quickly became a celebrity in Paris, appearing frequently in the press and drawing admirers like Robert de Montesquieu, that "precious arbiter elegantiarum of the period," as Benois called him.[169] She modeled herself on the famous actress Sarah Bernhardt, who became a friend and men-

Mme IDA RUBINSTEIN

tor. Rubinstein pursued love affairs with women as well as men including the artist Romaine Brooks, who painted a striking series of nude portraits of her, and Walter Guinness, the Anglo-Irish politician and beer magnate. She built a townhouse on the Place des États-Unis, purportedly kept leopards and panthers as pets (fig. 47), sailed the world in her yacht, and pursued her passion for big-game hunting in Africa.

After the successes of *Cléopâtre* and *Schéhérazade*, Diaghilev planned for Rubinstein to appear as the lead Nymph in Debussy's *L'Après-midi d'un Faune* and in other ballets. But Rubinstein, supported by her own wealth and by new patrons like Guinness, pursued her own path as an independent performer and producer. Asked years later why Rubinstein left the Ballets Russes, Léon Bakst, a good friend, cited an incident (perhaps anecdotal) in which the panther she kept as a pet, startled by Diaghilev's arrival to discuss her contract, leapt at him, forcing him onto a table. A deeper reason for their estrangement, however, was Rubinstein's independence, a quality Diaghilev could not easily abide in other people.[170]

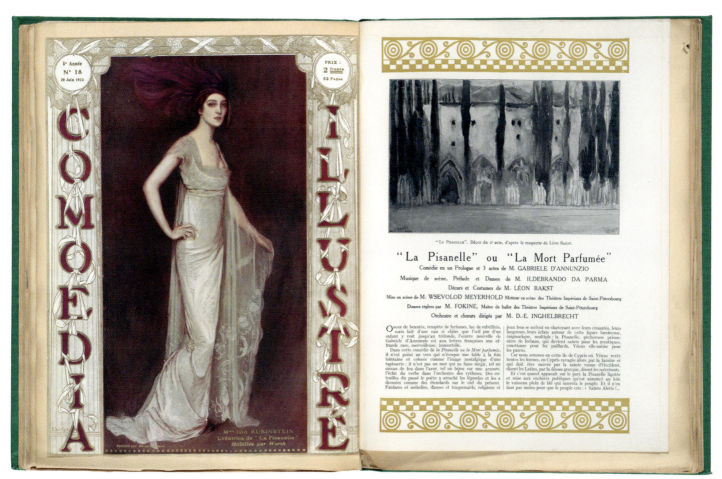

← **Fig. 47.** Ida Rubinstein with a leopard cub, [ca. 1910s]. Bibliothèque Nationale de France, Paris.

↑ **Fig. 48.** *Collection des plus beaux numéros de "Comoedia illustré" et des programmes consacrés aux ballets et galas russes depuis le début à Paris, 1909–1921.* The Morgan Library & Museum, New York, Mary Flagler Cary Music Collection. On left: Antonio de La Gándara (1861–1917), Portrait of Ida Rubinstein, 1913; right: Ida Rubinstein's 1913 production, *La Pisanelle*, with Bakst, Fokine, and D'Annunzio.

Saisons Russes in Paris, 1909–1921

Serge Diaghilev's and Ida Rubinstein's stage productions in the 1910s were celebrated alike in lavish souvenir programs published by *Comoedia illustré*. In a compilation for the years 1909–21, *Comoedia*'s editors discuss how they chose to present these "Saisons Russes" of both varieties—Diaghilev's ballets and Rubinstein's "galas" (genre-defying combinations of spoken word, singing, and dancing)—with equal billing. Many of the works that appeared in *Comoedia*, by both producers, featured Léon Bakst's designs.[171] The souvenir programs were expensive, their lavish presentation mixing stage designs and photographs of Rubinstein, Nijinsky, Karsavina, Stravinsky, Bakst, and other key figures, alongside advertisements for luxury products ranging from perfume and corsetry to restaurants and steam ships to New York.

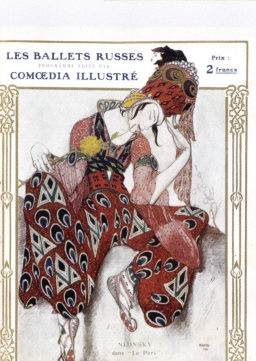

LES BALLETS RUSSES

Mme Karsavina et M. Forine dans L'Oiseau de Feu.

Mademoiselle N. Trouhanowa dans "LA PÉRI."

LES BALLETS RUSSES DE SERGE DE DIAGHILEW

1910
PARIS

THÉÂTRE DE L'OPÉRA

NOUVEAUX BALLETS

LE CARNAVAL
SCHÉHÉRAZADE
L'OISEAU DE FEU
GISÈLE

SPECTACLES DE GALA
DE
IDA RUBINSTEIN
1911

LE MARTYRE
DE SAINT SÉBASTIEN
MYSTÈRE EN CINQ ACTES
DE
GABRIELE D'ANNUNZIO
avec la musique de
CLAUDE DEBUSSY

Décors et Costumes de
LÉON BAKST

LEFT TO RIGHT

TOP ROW: Diaghilev's Saison Russe 1909, design by Léon Bakst; Ida Rubinstein in *Cléopâtre*, Ballets Russes 1909; Michel Fokine and Tamara Karsavina in *Firebird*, 1910; Natalia Trouhanova in *La Péri*, design by Léon Bakst, 1911.

MIDDLE ROW: Vaslav Nijinsky in *La Péri*, design by Léon Bakst, 1911; Caricatures by J. Dulac (clockwise): Maurice Ravel, Michel Fokine, Igor Stravinsky, Léon Bakst; Ida Rubinstein in *The Martyrdom of St. Sebastian*, produced by Rubinstein, 1911, illustration by Léon Bakst.

BOTTOM ROW: Cover of the 1909–21 *Comoedia illustré* compilation; Tamara Karsavina and Enrico Cecchetti in *Petrouchka*, 1911, costumes designed by Alexandre Benois; Vaslav Nijinsky and Tamara Karsavina in *Le Spectre de la Rose*, 1912 (left page) and *Carnaval*, 1910 (right page), drawings by Valentine Gross.

LEFT TO RIGHT

TOP ROW: Vaslav Nijinsky in *Le Spectre de la Rose*, 1912, drawing by Jean Cocteau; Vaslav Nijinsky in *Le Dieu Bleu*, 1912; *Le Dieu Bleu*, illustration by Léon Bakst, 1911; Ida Rubinstein in *Hélène de Sparte*, produced by Rubinstein, 1912, design by Léon Bakst.

MIDDLE ROW: Vaslav Nijinsky in *L'Après-midi d'un Faune*, 1912, design by Léon Bakst; Tamara Karsavina in *Le Coq d'Or*, 1914, drawing by Valentine Gross; *Le Tricorne*, 1919, curtain design by Pablo Picasso.

BOTTOM ROW: Portraits (clockwise): Pablo Picasso, Henri Matisse, Nicholas Roerich, Léon Bakst; Design for *Parade*, 1917, by Pablo Picasso; Design for *Le Tricorne*, 1919, by Pablo Picasso.

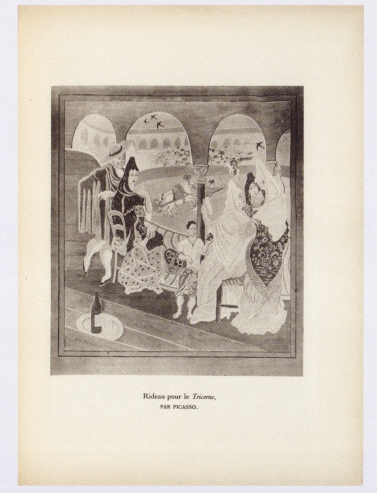

Rideau pour le *Tricorne*,
PAR PICASSO.

FOR THE NEXT three decades, Rubinstein single-mindedly pursued a life in the theater, producing a series of large-scale stage works with major writers, composers, choreographers, and visual artists of the day. With Gabriele D'Annunzio, Claude Debussy, Léon Bakst, and Michel Fokine, she produced *The Martyrdom of St. Sebastian* in 1911 (see fig. 20), starring as the male saint and attracting scandal when the archbishop of Paris threatened excommunication to anyone who attended.[172] In 1913 she produced and starred in *La Pisanelle*, again working with Gabriele D'Annunzio, Bakst, and Fokine (fig. 48). Nearly all her productions featured Bakst's designs, and the two remained devoted friends and collaborators until his death in 1924.

A 1926 biography offers one view of Rubinstein's public perception at the time, and a rare acknowledgement of the misogynist attitudes she dealt with throughout her career. "Mme Rubinstein inspires love or hate. . . . The dress rehearsal of a show she has put on is always feverish. . . . Some abandon themselves to transports of admiration and admit no reservations; others feel a strange fury rumbling in them. . . . She faces bizarre reproaches: Can we tolerate a woman giving herself the luxury of interpreting masterpieces? Is this not a scandal?"[173]

Whereas Diaghilev and his new cohort of artists, choreographers, and composers moved into the modernist aesthetics of the 1920s, Rubinstein kept to her original vision, pursuing a version of the Gesamtkunstwerk that remained closer to its roots in ancient Greek drama and the nineteenth-century Symbolist world of Baudelaire, Wagner, and Mallarmé. She expressed her artistic credo in a 1924 lecture titled "L'Art aux trois visages" (Art of Three Faces). Taking as her starting point Baudelaire's "famous sonnet" *Correspondances*, Rubinstein invoked Wagner's trinity of arts: music, dance, and poetry. Those individual art forms, Rubinstein believed, are merely different faces of an original, unified "*archi-art*," which serves not only as "the ornament and the crowning glory of existence," but, even more powerfully, as "a daily viaticum"—a vivid image: the viaticum is the sacrament a Catholic priest gives to a dying person. Art, Rubinstein declared, offers nothing less than *Revelation*, opening us to the voice of the divine; *Communion*, allowing us to collectively approach the eternal; and *Deliverance*, letting us escape our materialist, terrestrial life.[174] Rubinstein's lecture received high praise. A writer who attended observed: "This voice, resembling a song, astonished. Mme Ida Rubinstein combines intuition with real erudition. Archilochus is familiar to her. She's well versed in Aeschylus and Sophocles."[175]

In 1928 Ida Rubinstein fulfilled a long-held dream, launching a new ballet company, Les Ballets de Madame Ida Rubinstein (fig. 50). Her first call was to Alexandre Benois who, after Bakst died in 1924, became one of her most loyal collaborators. His vision for the future of ballet, since his youthful encounter with Tchaikovsky's *Sleeping Beauty*, had helped to inspire the founding of the Ballets Russes.[176] For Rubinstein's new company Benois served as her designer and artistic confidant, reprising the role he had played at Diaghilev's side from the 1890s. He created the stage designs and libretti for nearly every production, worked with the choreographers and composers, and oversaw all the elements of each work, making sure they fused harmoniously[177]—echoing the Gesamtkunstwerk ideal of a unified artwork that had guided the early years of the Ballets Russes. Rubinstein drew an all-star team of Ballets Russes alumni, including not only herself and Benois but Stravinsky and Ravel, as well as two of Diaghilev's choreographers, Léonide Massine and Bronislava Nijinska.

Nijinska hired and directed the dancers, and choreographed seven of the nine ballets planned for the first 1928–29 season. Whereas Diaghilev's Ballets Russes was notably male-dominated, including few women in any role, Rubinstein's new ballet enterprise featured female protagonists—not only Rubinstein herself, but also central roles for women in creative

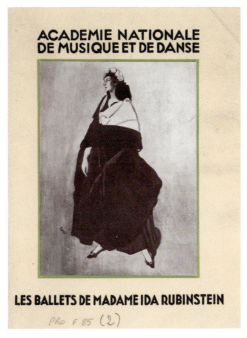

← **Fig. 49.** Léon Bakst (1866–1924), *Mme Ida Rubinstein*, 1917. The Metropolitan Museum of Art, New York, the Chester Dale Collection, 1962.
↑ **Fig. 50.** Program for *Bolero* premiere, November 1928.

and administrative positions including Nijinska, the artist Hélène Benois (Alexandre's daughter) as one of the company's chief scene painters, and others.[178] The company was notably international, including dancers from England, Denmark, Romania, Poland, the United States, and Bulgaria, as well as numerous Russian émigrés,[179] prefiguring the "international" companies that made their mark in the 1930s.[180]

Planning the new company's first season, Rubinstein and Benois spent evenings together dreaming up ideas for the ballets they would produce, listening to the pianist Marcelle Atoch playing Bach, Schubert, Liszt, and Debussy, as well as Maurice Ravel's *Le Tombeau de Couperin*, a 1914–17 piano work that had been adapted as a ballet in 1920.[181] Benois revived ballet scenarios he had long imagined, some of which he had proposed for Diaghilev's company years before, which had never been produced.[182]

WANTING A NEWLY commissioned ballet by Ravel, Rubinstein asked the composer for a score on a Spanish theme. The concept may hark back to Ravel's friendship with Benois, in the early years of the Ballets Russes, and their mutual love for Spain. They went on a beach trip in 1914 (accompanied by their mothers) to collaborate on a Spanish-themed ballet (fig. 51), but World War I interrupted their plans.[183] The Spanish connection ran deep for Ravel, whose mother was of Basque heritage,[184] and expressed itself in many of his works including *L'Heure espagnole* and *Rapsodie espagnole*.[185]

Now, fourteen years later, Rubinstein's new ballet company offered the chance to realize their idea. Rubinstein asked Ravel to orchestrate parts of *Iberia* by the Spanish composer Isaac Albéniz, but after finding out in June 1928, just months before the premiere, that the score had already been arranged by another musician with exclusive rights for a ballet, Ravel felt compelled to compose an original score instead.[186] He completed *Bolero* in haste and under great stress between July and October 1928,[187] and Ida Rubinstein's company premiered the ballet in November with Rubinstein in the lead role, choreography by Bronislava Nijinska, and stage designs by Alexandre Benois.

Ravel's famous score (see pp. 106–7) draws together threads that weave through his music as a whole. His affinity for Spanish culture expresses itself in the rhythm he used as a starting point for the work,

↑　**Fig. 51.** Alexandre Benois (1870–1960), Sketch of Maurice Ravel at the beach, Saint-Jean-de-Luz, July 1914. Bibliothèque Nationale de France, Paris.
→　**Fig. 52.** Elliott & Fry (act. 1863–1962), Portrait of Maurice Ravel, inscribed to Louise Alvar, 23 October 1928, shortly after completing *Bolero*. The Morgan Library & Museum, New York, bequest of Charles Alvar Harding, 2001.

referencing a traditional slow triple-meter couple's dance to guitar and castanets. Just as important to the composer's conception was his interest in the workings of machines, which went back to his father. Joseph Ravel, whose career was in the developing automobile industry, took his sons to see factories.[188] Maurice's abiding interest in mechanical things showed in works like his early piano masterpiece *Jeux d'eau* (*Fountains*),[189] which seems to evoke a fountain controlled by a sophisticated algorithm.[190] On a concert tour to the United States a few months before he composed *Bolero*, Ravel visited the Ford motor factory in Detroit,[191] later explaining that "it was a factory that inspired my *Boléro*. I would like it always to be played with a vast factory in the background."[192]

For some listeners, *Bolero* suggests sexual tension and release. After fifteen minutes of music in a single, unchanging key, the music suddenly shifts to a new harmony shortly before the end, followed by a dramatic outburst of loud brass instruments. As musicologist Deborah Mawer notes, "Death, mechanical explosion, or orgasm: the raison d'être of *Boléro* is its cataclysmic destruction as the culmination of an extended trajectory . . . the irrevocable, dissonant rupture occurs six bars from the finish. . . . The ultimate gesture only works because the preceding order has been so rigorous and its timespan so over-extended."[193]

Bolero stands as an early masterpiece of repetitive music, perhaps prefiguring the minimalism that later transformed European-American concert music in the work of composers like Philip Glass and John Adams. A review of the ballet's first performance captured Ravel's achievement: "All the skill of our classical rhetoric would be incapable of making us accept twenty rhythmic, melodic, and contrapuntal variations on a theme of this kind: Ravel found a way not only to avoid all monotony, but to arouse a constantly growing interest until the end, by repeating his theme twenty times like a frieze motif, by asking for twenty lighting changes from the sheer magic of color, which lead us, amazed, from one end to the other of this musical paradox."[194]

Music, Dance, and Design—*Bolero*

Ravel saw *Bolero* as a musical experiment in which he would keep the material simple to an extreme degree. In a letter to a friend in September 1928, while secluded at home frantically working on the manuscript, the composer described his work in progress: "no music, no composition, just an orchestra display."[195] He would employ none of the methods a classical composer typically uses to vary and develop their material. Instead, his composing manuscripts for the work, including early pencil sketches and the full orchestral score (which he dedicated on the first page to Ida Rubinstein, the ballet's commissioner, producer, and lead dancer) show his plan to repeat the spare, beguiling melody a predetermined number of times.[196] The only changing element would be the orchestration, gradually growing bigger and louder as more instruments joined in. In effect, his piece sets in motion a mechanical process and leaves it to unfold as if without human intervention, like a factory production line (see Ravel's interest in factories and mechanics, p. 105).

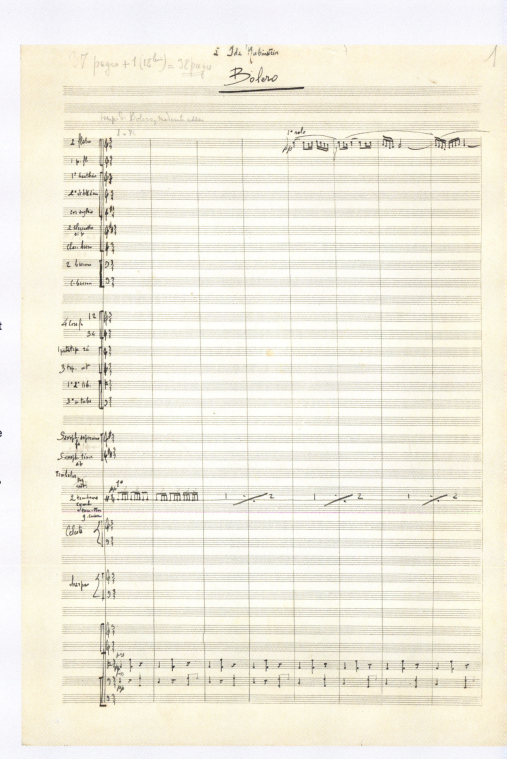

Maurice Ravel (1875–1937), *Bolero*, autograph manuscript, full score, first and
last pages (pp. 1 and 37), 1928. Dedication
on first page "to Ida Rubinstein." The
Morgan Library & Museum, New York,
Robert Owen Lehman Collection, on
deposit.

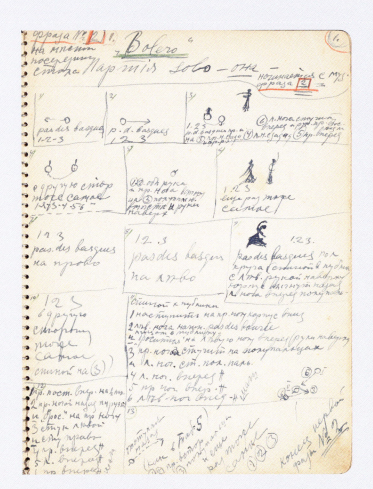

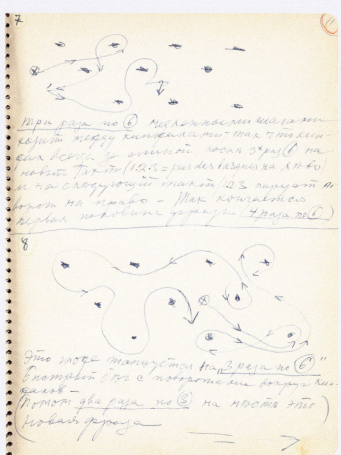

Bronislava Nijinska (1891–1972), Notebook
containing choreographic notes and
drawings for *Bolero*, pp. 1 and 11, [1928].
Library of Congress, Bronislava Nijinska
Collection.

Nijinska traced her choreography in *Bolero* directly to her earlier innovations: "*Les Noces* is the basis, the beginning of a series of my ballets created in the form of a symphonic sonata. . . . *Les Biches* 1924, *Le Train Bleu* 1924 . . . *Bolero* 1928. . . ."[197] During her rehearsals for *Bolero*'s 1928 premiere, an observer noted how she kept on the piano "an enormous file of annotations on loose sheets, sketches, and diagrams. She consults them before giving the least direction to her dancers."[198] One of the notebooks she used for *Bolero* offers a sense of the detail in which she captured her ideas on paper. The first page shows a sequence of numbered steps at the beginning of the ballet. At middle-right on the page, at box "9," Nijinska draws a figure with arm raised, noting "Basque steps, walk a demi-tour (back to audience)[,] with left arm raised, throw the upper body back[,] the left foot forward and in demi-pointe."[199] She annotates the floor path drawn at the top of page 11, beginning "Three times (6) Walk slowly between the daggers[,] For each time a dagger remains behind your back . . ."[200]

Alexandre Benois's designs for the ballet evoked an imagined Spanish tavern and its clientele. His concept referenced the Romantic-era Spanish artist Francisco Goya, some elements copied almost directly.[201] Praised as one of his greatest achievements,[202] Benois's designs for *Bolero* reflected his knowledge of eighteenth-century art.

The large table on which Ida Rubinstein danced may have been Nijinska's idea, perhaps inspired by a postcard she kept in her archive. Benois made the table central to his conception for the ballet.

ABOVE LEFT: Francisco Goya (1746–1828), Plate 5 from *Los Caprichos*, 1799. The Metropolitan Museum of Art, New York, gift of M. Knoedler & Co., 1918.

ABOVE RIGHT: Alexandre Benois (1870–1960), Costume design for La Maja in *Bolero*, 1928. Collection of Paul Stiga.

FAR LEFT: "Costumbres Andaluzas." Postcard, n.d. Library of Congress, Bronislava Nijinska Collection.

MIDDLE LEFT: Alexandre Benois (1870–1960), Stage design for *Bolero*, [1928]. Bibliothèque Nationale de France, Paris.

LEFT: Ida Rubinstein with cast on stage in *Bolero*, 1928. Library of Congress, Ida Rubinstein Collection.

Bolero's premiere on 22 November 1928, the new company's opening night, unfolded on the grand stage of the Paris Opéra, where Rubinstein had seen one of her early triumphs two decades before, in *Schéhérazade* with the Ballets Russes. The scenario Rubinstein and Nijinska created for *Bolero* was simple. Like *L'Après-midi d'un Faune*, it is an evocation of a scene more than a story. A critic captured the effect:

> a Spanish-style tavern, but fantastic . . . oversize table and lamp, and in the shadowy recesses the silhouettes of muleteers and smugglers, acclaiming the dancer in a black bodice on the table, who, in her sheath of light, without lascivious writhings or provocative gestures indicates the movement of the dance that transports her; she does not seem to see them; without swirling shawls or flashy jewels, she attends only to the call of the music, which is the soul of the dance. The fascinated groups clap their hands, spring to life, and spin around the table always dominated by this tall figure whose inner energy creates the rhythmic twisting that magnetizes the space [see pp. 108–9].[203]

Serge Diaghilev, with an eye on the competition, hurried back from England to catch a performance. In the prewar years he had viewed Rubinstein as a rival when she presented *The Martyrdom of St. Sebastian* in 1911 and other works. Now he saw her ballet company as a new threat, with its unlimited budget, lavish productions,[204] access to the city's most prestigious venue (which the Ballets Russes could not always afford), and team of top talent, many of whom had worked for him previously. Diaghilev's withering comments betrayed his bitterness: the ballet was "nothing but provincial boredom," Rubinstein's performance a "total failure," and Nijinska's choreography "just a lot of running about, sloppiness. . . ."[205]

The impresario's sour response could not diminish *Bolero*'s success. The applause was thunderous, and the extensive press coverage was enthusiastic. Ravel's score quickly became a staple of the concert hall, reaching a level of popularity rare in classical music. He was happily surprised, after a radio broadcast of the work, to walk past a construction site and hear workers whistling the tune.[206] Nijinska revived the ballet in 1932 for her company Théâtre de la Danse Nijinska with herself in the lead role and stage designs by Natalia Goncharova, her collaborator from *Les Noces*.[207] Some of Nijinska's choreographic ideas, including the large table (see

← **Fig. 53.** *Bolero* in rehearsal, 1928. Studio des Champs-Élysées, Paris. At center: Anatole Viltzak, Ida Rubinstein's co-lead. Library of Congress, Bronislava Nijinska Collection.

↑ **Fig. 54.** Alexandre Benois (1870–1960), Costume design for the Matador in *Bolero*, 1928; with fabric swatches (at left). The New York Public Library, Jerome Robbins Dance Division.

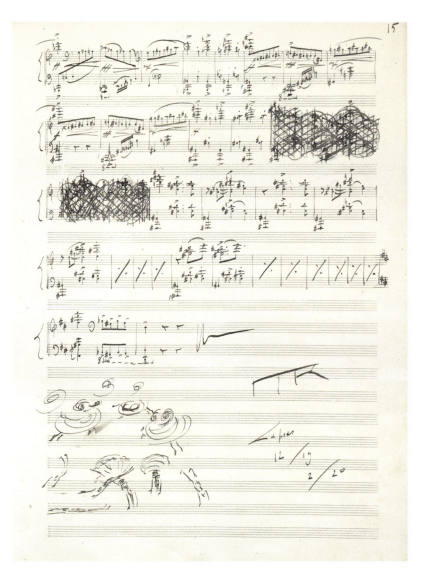

pp. 108–109), were taken up by the choreographer Maurice Béjart in his 1961 production of *Bolero*. The work is heard most often today in the concert hall, and in innumerable adaptations, recordings, and films. Its origin as a ballet, and the roles Ida Rubinstein, Alexandre Benois, and Bronislava Nijinska played in its creation, are little known today.

IDA RUBINSTEIN STAGED two other notable ballets during her first 1928–29 season. Ravel had composed *La Valse* in 1919–20 for Diaghilev, anticipating imminent performance by the Ballets Russes, even adding doodles of dancing figures on the final page (fig. 55). But when Ravel played the score for Diaghilev, the impresario dismissed it as "a masterpiece" but "not a ballet," offending the composer and ending their relationship.[208] Rubinstein may have taken some pleasure in giving Ravel's score its first major ballet production, in 1929, once more with designs by Benois and choreography by Nijinska (figs. 56, 57).[209]

Rubinstein cemented her stance as rival to Diaghilev when she commissioned Igor Stravinsky, who had remained close to the Ballets Russes ever since *Firebird*, to compose a new ballet for her company, *Le Baiser de la Fée* (*The Fairy's Kiss*), which she premiered with *Bolero* in November 1928. Benois, drawing on his lifelong love of Tchaikovsky, proposed a set of the composer's melodies, which Stravinsky recomposed as a new work based on a story by Hans Christian Andersen.[210] Their collaboration was a reunion of sorts, almost two decades after the two had created *Petrouchka* for the Ballets Russes in 1911.

Rubinstein's ballet company differed in many ways from Diaghilev's. Hers was not a continuous operation like the Ballets Russes, disbanding and reassembling repeatedly between 1929 and 1934. In 1934, Rubinstein hired Michel Fokine, Diaghilev's first choreographer, to stage several ballets and Stravinsky to stage a new collaboration with the writer André Gide, *Perséphone*.[211] Her final project, Paul Claudel's *Jeanne d'Arc au Bûcher* with music by Arthur Honegger, premiered in 1938 on the eve of World War II.[212]

Bronislava Nijinska's work in Ida Rubinstein's productions had a tremendous impact on one of the young dancers she hired for the company, Frederick Ashton, who would become one of the twentieth century's leading choreographers. Her method of grouping dancers into architectonic shapes influenced his choreography for a 1935 London production of *Le Baiser de la Fée* starring Margot

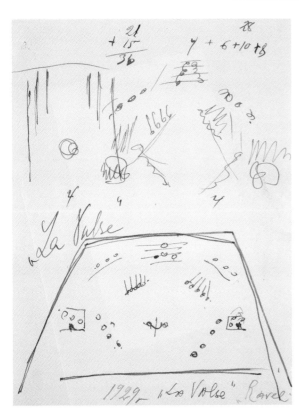

↖ **Fig. 55.** Maurice Ravel (1875–1937), *La Valse*, autograph manuscript, solo piano, p. 15, 1920. The Morgan Library & Museum, New York, Mary Flagler Cary Music Collection, gift of Robert Owen Lehman. The final page features Ravel's drawings of waltzing couples.

↑ **Fig. 56.** Bronislava Nijinska (1891–1972), Sketch for *La Valse* showing the stage with dancers' positions, 1929. Library of Congress, Bronislava Nijinska Collection.

← **Fig. 57.** Alexandre Benois (1870–1960), Scene design for *La Valse* with conductor and dancing couples, 1930. Harvard Theatre Collection, Houghton Library.

Fonteyn; his elongated, asymmetrical group formation from the fourth tableau (fig. 58) is strongly reminiscent of Nijinska's formations in *Les Noces*.[213] When Ashton was director of the Royal Ballet he invited her to restage two of her masterpieces, *Les Biches* in 1964 and *Les Noces* in 1966. The revivals were revelatory, rekindling Nijinska's international reputation near the end of her life (see p. 95).

Nijinska worked for Rubinstein until June 1929, and again in 1931. She later moved to the United States, settling in Hollywood, California, in 1940 (where Stravinsky also settled the following year) and maintaining a busy career as choreographer and teacher until her death in 1972— though she received far less recognition than other Diaghilev protégés, particularly his last choreographer, George Balanchine. Alexandre Benois enjoyed a long career, producing stage works until his death in 1960, at age ninety. Ida Rubinstein continued producing new works through the 1930s, always playing the leading roles. Following their collaboration on *Bolero*, Ravel and Rubinstein became close friends and planned new projects, including a ballet, *Morgiane*, on a story from the *Thousand and One Nights*, a work which was never written due to the onset of the cognitive illness that would end Ravel's life in 1937.[214] Ida Rubinstein spent the last decade of her life in seclusion, her celebrity fading to obscurity before her death in 1960. An obituary was titled "Une inconnue jadis célèbre": An unknown, once celebrated.[215]

IN THE CLOSING chapter of this story, many of its key figures, whose creative ideals guided artistic developments of the time—Rubinstein, Benois, Nijinska, Ravel, Stravinsky—joined forces in a potent combination in Rubinstein's ballet company. Their new ballets of the late 1920s and early 1930s reclaimed and reframed the Romantic impulse; Nijinska's neoclassical innovations, which she expanded beyond her brother Nijinsky's modernist experiments, now gave way to a new Romanticism, recombining elements of what had come before—the thrall of Symbolism, its expansion in modernist trends toward abstraction, and a return to the balletic "smile" of the spirit that Benois had envisioned from his youth—a delight which, as he believed, ballet was the art form best suited to bestow (see p. 43). Ballets like *Bolero* introduced new musical possibilities that would be borne out through the twentieth century.

Ida Rubinstein's ballet company was an early example of the kind of international enterprise that would come to prominence with the post-Diaghilev companies. The music she commissioned echoes in the repertories of companies like Sadler's Wells and the New York City Ballet, which coalesced along national lines in the 1930s and 1940s. Both Frederick

↑ **Fig. 58.** Frederick Ashton's 1935 choreography for the fourth tableau of Stravinsky's *Le Baiser de la Fée*. Photograph by J. W. Debenham, from *Frederick Ashton and His Ballets* by David Vaughan.

↙ **Fig. 59.** Program for Les Ballets de Madame Ida Rubinstein. Académie Nationale de Musique et de Danse, May 1929. Library of Congress, Ida Rubinstein Collection.

↓ **Fig. 60.** Flyer for Les Ballets de Madame Ida Rubinstein, featuring *Bolero*, *La Valse*, *Perséphone*, etc., 1934. Library of Congress, Ida Rubinstein Collection.

MADAME IDA RUBINSTIN

THÉATRE NATIONAL DE L'OPÉRA

LES BALLETS
DE
Mme IDA RUBINSTEIN

LES 30 AVRIL, 4 & 9 MAI	LES 11, 16 & 21 MAI
PREMIÈRE REPRÉSENTATION	PREMIÈRE REPRÉSENTATION
DIANE DE POITIERS	**ORIANE LA SANS ÉGALE**
Livret de Mme Elisabeth de GRAMMONT	Livret de M. Claude SERAN
Chorégraphie de M. Michel FOKINE	Chorégraphie de M. Michel FOKINE
Musique de M. Jacques IBERT	Musique de M. Florent SCHMITT
PREMIÈRE REPRÉSENTATION	PREMIÈRE REPRÉSENTATION
PERSEPHONE	**SEMIRAMIS**
Poème de M. André GIDE	Poème de M. Paul VALÉRY
Chorégraphie de M. Kurt JOOSS	Chorégraphie de M. Michel FOKINE
Musique de M. Igor STRAWINSKI	Musique de M. Arthur HONEGGER
LA VALSE	**BOLERO**
Chorégraphie de M. Michel FOKINE	Chorégraphie de M. Michel FOKINE
Musique de M. Maurice RAVEL	Musique de M. Maurice RAVEL

Chef d'Orchestre : M. Gustave CLOEZ
Metteur en Scène : M. Jacques COPEAU

Décors et Costumes de MM. Alexandre BENOIS, Alexandre JAKOVLEV, Pedro PRUNA et André BARSACQ.
Décors exécutés par MM. Georges MOUVEAU et Nicolas BENOIS.

Ashton and George Balanchine, who launched his career as Diaghilev's last choreographer, would create versions of Ravel's *La Valse* and Stravinsky's *Le Baiser de la Fée*, and Balanchine enjoyed a famous series of collaborations with Stravinsky. The Rubinstein company nurtured a new generation of Russian émigré dancers, trained in the Paris studios of former Maryinsky ballerinas.

The most far-reaching legacy of these ballets remains the music, alive in the manuscripts of the Robert Owen Lehman Collection. Diaghilev's Ballets Russes and Les Ballets de Madame Ida Rubinstein show their deepest impact in the scores they commissioned from Stravinsky, Debussy, Ravel, and most of the other leading composers of the time. Works like *Firebird*, *Prélude à l'après-midi d'un faune*, *The Rite of Spring*, *Les Noces*, *Bolero*, and *La Valse* not only continue to inspire new ballet productions, but remain staples of the concert hall, filled with tunes instantly recognizable to many even casual music lovers.

Epigraph. Jean-Georges Noverre, as quoted in S. L. Grigoriev, *The Diaghilev Ballet, 1909–1929*, ed. and trans. Vera Bowen (London: Constable, 1953), 46.

1   Davinia Caddy, *Ballets Russes and Beyond: Music and Dance in Belle-Époque Paris* (Cambridge: Cambridge University Press, 2012), 29. The decline concerned the intellectual prestige of ballet, particularly ballet performed on the opera-house stage as opposed to the numerous ballets produced throughout Europe at music-hall venues.

2   Alexandre Benois, *Reminiscences of the Russian Ballet*, trans. Mary Britnieva (New York: Da Capo Press, 1977), 130–31, 373.

3   Alexandre Benois, "Beseda o balete" [Colloquy on ballet], in V. Meyerhold et al., *Teatr* (St. Petersburg: Shipnovik, 1908), 100.

4   Alexandre Benois, "The Origins of the Ballets Russes," in Boris Kochno, *Diaghilev and the Ballets Russes*, trans. Adrienne W. Foulke (New York: Harper & Row, 1970), 5.

5   Sjeng Scheijen, *Diaghilev: A Life*, trans. Jane Hedley-Prôle and S. J. Leinbach (Oxford: Oxford University Press, 2009), 170.

6   Benois, "Origins of the Ballets Russes," 16.

7   Juliet Bellow, *Modernism on Stage: The Ballets Russes and the Parisian Avant-Garde* (New York: Ashgate, 2013), 11–12.

8   Tamara Karsavina became the Ballets Russes' prima ballerina, starring in *Firebird* and many other productions. Benois recalled how "the success of our performances depended in large part on her." Benois, "Origins of the Ballets Russes," 18.

9   Michel Fokine, "The New Russian Ballet," *The Times* (London), 6 July 1914, 6.

10   Lubov Blok, *Klassicheskii tanets: istoria i sovremennost'* [Classical dance: History and modernity], ed. Vadim Gaevsky and Elizabeth Souritz (Moscow: Iskusstvo, 1987). Quoted in Elizabeth Souritz, "Isadora Duncan and Prewar Russian Dancemakers," in *The Ballets Russes and Its World*, ed. Lynn Garafola and Nancy Van Norman Baer (New Haven: Yale University Press, 1999), 110.

11   Following *Schéhérazade*'s premiere, "dresses made of brightly colored oriental silks appeared in all the Maisons de Couture, and women started to wear oriental turbans decorated with jewels. . . . Maison Poiret gained a reputation for its oriental styles and the bright oriental colors of its dress designs." Bronislava Nijinska, *Early Memoirs*, ed. and trans. Irina Nijinska and Jean Rawlinson, introd. Anna Kisselgoff (Durham: Duke University Press, 1981), 297.

12   Stephen Walsh, *Debussy: A Painter in Sound* (New York: Alfred A. Knopf, 2018), 199.

13   François Lesure, *Claude Debussy: A Critical Biography*, ed. and trans. Marie Rolf (Rochester, NY: University of Rochester Press, 2019), 254.

14   Scheijen, *Diaghilev*, 191. Although *Firebird* was Stravinsky's first major Diaghilev commission, he had worked for the Ballets Russes for its previous season, orchestrating Frédéric Chopin's *Valse*, Op. 18 for a movement of the Ballets Russes' 1909 ballet *Les Sylphides*. Chopin's autograph manuscript of Op. 18 is held in the Robert Owen Lehman Collection on deposit at the Morgan Library & Museum.

15   Michel Fokine, *Memoirs of a Ballet Master*, ed. Anatole Chujoy, trans. Vitale Fokine (Boston: Little, Brown and Company, 1961), 161.

16   Grigoriev, 32.

17   Igor Stravinsky, *L'Oiseau de feu: Fac-simile du manuscrit Saint-Pétersbourg, 1909–1910*, studies and commentary by Louis Cyr, Jean-Jacques Eigeldinger, and Pierre Wissmer (Geneva: Conservatoire de Musique de Genève / Minkoff, 1985), 180.

18   Compared with Bakst's approach, Alexandre Benois's costume designs (pp. 109, 111) provide more practical detail for the costume maker.

19   Sarah Woodcock, "Wardrobe," in *Diaghilev and the Golden Age of the Ballets Russes*, ed. Jane Pritchard, exh. cat. (London: V&A Publishing, 2010), 143.

20   Richard Taruskin, *Stravinsky and the Russian Traditions: A Biography of the Works through "Mavra,"* vol. 1 (Berkeley: University of California Press, 1996), 498–99.

21   Kessler to Hofmannsthal, 5 June 1909. Hugo von Hofmannsthal and Harry Graf Kessler, *Briefwechsel* (Frankfurt: Insel Verlag, 1968), 239–40. Quoted in Scheijen, *Diaghilev*, 184.

22   More typically at the time, stage designs for ballet were created by teams of scene painters specializing in specific subject matter (palaces, gardens, interiors, etc.), each working on separate elements of a production with no overall guiding design concept.

23   Igor Stravinsky, *An Autobiography* [1936] (London: Calder & Boyars, 1975), 82. Quoted in Stephanie Jordan, *Stravinsky Dances: Re-Visions across a Century* (Alton, UK: Dance Books, 2007), 94.

24   Lynn Garafola, *Diaghilev's Ballets Russes* (New York: Oxford University Press, 1989), 10.

25   Charles Joseph, "Diaghilev and Stravinsky," in Garafola and Baer, *The Ballets Russes and Its World*, 193–94.

26   Diaghilev originally intended Anna Pavlova for the role of the Firebird. She starred in the first 1909 season, and Diaghilev planned to feature her in the 1910 season (fig. 2). When she dropped out, Tamara Karsavina took over the role.

27   Tamara Karsavina, *Theatre Street: The Reminiscences of Tamara Karsavina* (London: William Heinemann, 1930), 261.

28   For Stravinsky's use of the pianola, partly for control of tempo, in *Les Noces* and other works, see p. 87.

29   Stravinsky, *L'Oiseau de feu: Fac-simile*, 192.

30   Charles Joseph, "Stravinsky Manuscripts in the Library of Congress and the Pierpont Morgan Library," *The Journal of Musicology* 1, no. 3 (July 1982): 330.

31   Jordan, *Stravinsky Dances*, 29.

32   The extant notations in Fokine's hand for *Firebird* include cast lists, a rehearsal schedule for March 1910, and dance drawings for specific scenes. Described in Claudia Jeschke and Nicole Haitzinger, *Schwäne und Feuervögel: Die Ballets Russes, 1909–1929. Russische Bildwelten in Bewegung* ([Leipzig]: Henschel, [2009]), 68.

33   Jeschke and Haitzinger, *Schwäne und Feuervögel*, 70–71.

34   Quoted in Cyril W. Beaumont, *Michel Fokine and His Ballets* (New York: Dance Horizons, 1981), 23.

35   Alexandre Benois, "Khudozhestvennye pis'ma" [Art letter], *Rech*, 12 July 1910. Trans. in Roland John Wiley, "Benois' Commentaries—Part III on the First Saisons Russes," *Dancing Times*, December 1980.

36   Peter Lieven, *The Birth of the Ballets-Russes* (New York: Dover Publications, 1973), 131.

37   Richard Taruskin, "The Antiliterary Man: Diaghilev and Music," in Nancy Van Norman Baer, ed., *The Art of Enchantment: Diaghilev's Ballets Russes, 1909–1929*, exh. cat. (San Francisco: Fine Arts Museums of San Francisco; New York: Universe Books, 1988), 118.

38   Taruskin, *Stravinsky and the Russian Traditions*, 662.

39   Ibid., 717. Regarding musical sources for *Petrouchka*, see Taruskin, 695–717.

40   The Lehman Collection on deposit at the Morgan Library also holds Stravinsky's autograph manuscript of his 1946 revision of the work.

41   Scheijen, *Diaghilev*, 211.

42   Taruskin, *Stravinsky and the Russian Traditions*, 662–63.

43   Ibid., 664–65. The Juilliard Manuscript Collection holds Stravinsky's manuscript sketches for *Petrouchka* dated 11 June 1910, which seem to resemble music conceived for

a piano concerto, though they include annotations such as "Arab" indicating similarities to the eventual ballet version. Among the sketches is music for tableaux 1–3, including passages that do not appear in the later ballet version. See https://juilliardmanuscriptcollection.org/petrushka-sketches.

44 Awkwardly, Diaghilev had recently alienated Benois, his old friend and collaborator, by publicly crediting Bakst with the conception of *Schéhérazade* in 1910 rather than Benois, who claimed to be its true author. Taruskin, *Stravinsky and the Russian Traditions*, 663, 670.

45 Benois's authorship of *Petrouchka* was later obscured, first when he understated his own role in a 1911 article (*Rech*, 4 August 1911, trans. in Roland John Wiley, *Dancing Times*, April 1981, 464) and in later years when Stravinsky would attempt to minimize his contribution, even suing him in 1929 to end the royalties Benois received for performances. Taruskin, *Stravinsky and the Russian Traditions*, 671.

46 Taruskin, *Stravinsky and the Russian Traditions*, 673. This may reflect Benois's deep knowledge of the eighteenth century. The Tiepolo family's *Punchinello* drawings (of which the Morgan Library holds a significant collection) began to merge Punch and Pierrot. St. Petersburg's Butter Week with its pierogis is akin to Italy's Carnival and its gnocchi.

47 Ibid., 680.

48 Karsavina, *Theatre Street*, 243.

49 Fokine, "New Russian Ballet," 6.

50 Fokine, *Memoirs of a Ballet Master*, 183. He references the principles he laid out in his 1914 letter to the London *Times* (see p. 45).

51 Igor Stravinsky, *Dialogi* (Leningrad: [n.p.], 1971), 68. Trans. in Igor Stravinsky and Robert Craft, *Dialogues* (Garden City, NY: Doubleday, 1963).

52 In 1921, reclaiming *Petrouchka*'s origins as a concert piece for piano, Stravinsky arranged three movements for the pianist Arthur Rubinstein, a work that remains popular in concert halls today. The autograph manuscript is held in the Robert Owen Lehman Collection on deposit at the Morgan Library & Museum.

53 During the Ballets Russes 1916 tour of the United States, authorities asked for cuts to *Schéhérazade* when American audiences could not abide the sight of a man in dark body paint engaged in sexual encounter with a white woman. Garafola, "The Ballets Russes in America," in Baer, *Art of Enchantment*, 128.

54 [Fernand] Nozière, *Ida Rubinstein, Les célébrités de la scène française*, ed. R. Chiberre (Paris: Éditions Sansot, 1926), 19.

55 Bellow, *Modernism on Stage*, 47–48.

56 Caddy, *Ballets Russes and Beyond*, 30–31.

57 Eric Lott, in his study of American blackface minstrelsy, notes the "dialectical flickering of racial insult and racial envy" inherent in the practice, a thread which, though removed in time and place from Paris of the Belle Époque, likewise runs through the racialized exoticism found in the Ballets Russes and its time. Lott, *Love and Theft: Blackface Minstrelsy and the American Working Class* [1993] (Oxford: Oxford University Press, 2013), 18.

58 Oakland Ballet in 1991 cast the Moor in blue face paint. Isabelle Fokine, granddaughter of Michel Fokine, the ballet's choreographer, has suggested recasting the character as a "Warrior" whose aggressive and lustful persona matches his role in the story. Wendy Perron, "It's Time to Overhaul the Blackface (or Blueface) Puppet in *Petrouchka*," *Dance Magazine*, 14 July 2020, https://www.dancemagazine.com/blackface-in-ballet, viewed 31 August 2023.

59 Alexandre Stipanovich, "Meet Kandis Williams and Her Dancing Bodies," *Interview Magazine*, 29 December 2021. Also see Georgina Pazcoguin's *Swan Dive: The Making of a Rogue Ballerina* (New York: Henry Holt and Company, 2021).

60 This is according to Léon Bakst, in an interview with Louis Thomas, "Le peintre Bakst parle de Madame Ida Rubinstein," *La Revue critique des idées et des livres* 36, no. 221 (February 1924): 96.

61 According to Diaghilev's black notebook, in which he kept planning notes from 1910 to 1911. Jane Pritchard, "Creating Productions," in Pritchard, *Diaghilev and the Golden Age of the Ballets Russes*, 71–72.

62 Lesure, *Debussy*, 278.

63 Scheijen, *Diaghilev*, 233, 251. As part of his effort to bring a more modern aspect to his company, in 1913 Diaghilev began planning a new ballet with music by Arnold Schoenberg. He met the Austrian composer, who was then not well known in France, and heard a performance of *Pierrot Lunaire*, one of Schoenberg's defining atonal works (Scheijen, *Diaghilev*, 258–59). Schoenberg's autograph manuscript of *Pierrot* is held in the Robert Owen Lehman Collection on deposit at the Morgan Library.

64 Walsh, *Debussy*, 74.

65 Mallarmé's first 1876 edition of *L'Après-midi d'un faune* is held at the Morgan Library & Museum.

66 Claude Debussy to Henri Gauthier-Villars, 10 October 1896. *Debussy Letters*, ed. François Lesure and Roger Nichols, trans. Roger Nichols (Cambridge, MA: Harvard University Press, 1987), 84.

67 See Marie Rolf, "Debussy's Rites of Spring," in *Rethinking Debussy*, ed. Elliott Antokoletz and Marianne Wheeldon (New York: Oxford University Press, 2011). Autograph manuscripts of two of these early works are held in the Morgan Library's music manuscripts collection: *Le Printemps (Salut, printemps)* (1882) and *Printemps* (1884) were each written for preliminary rounds of the Prix de Rome.

68 Lesure, *Debussy*, 85. The first 1890 edition of Debussy's *Cinq poèmes de Ch. Baudelaire*, inscribed in his hand to the composer Erik Satie, is in the Morgan's music collection, PMM 276.

69 Ibid., 112–13.

70 Marie Rolf, "Oriental and Iberian Resonances in Early Debussy Songs," in *Debussy's Resonance*, ed. François de Médicis and Steven Huebner (Rochester, NY: University of Rochester Press, 2018), 273.

71 Annegret Fauser, *Musical Encounters at the 1889 Paris World's Fair* (Rochester, NY: University of Rochester Press, 2005), 198–99.

72 Quoted in Edward Lockspeiser, *Debussy: His Life and Mind*, vol. 1 (London: Cassell, 1962), 208.

73 *Prélude à l'après-midi d'un faune: Fac-similé du manuscrit autographe de la partition d'orchestre*, vol. 1 of *De main de maître* (Paris: Bibliothèque Nationale de France; Turnhout: Brepols Publishers, 2014), 6.

74 Claude Debussy, *Prélude à l'après-midi d'un faune*. Autograph manuscript, full score. Bibliothèque Nationale de France, Paris, Musique Ms 17685, 26.

75 Marie Rolf, "Orchestral Manuscripts of Claude Debussy: 1892–1905," *The Musical Quarterly* 70, no. 4 (Autumn 1984): 546.

76 Douglas Woodfull-Harris, ed., *Prelude à l'après-midi d'un faune*. Bärenreiter Urtext Edition (Kassel, Germany: Bärenreiter, 2001), iii.

77 Translation by Robinson McClellan.

78 Rolf, "Orchestral Manuscripts of Claude Debussy," 544.

79 According to Bronislava Nijinska (*Early Memoirs*, 292).

80 See the 2019 exhibition catalogue edited by Clare Fitzgerald, *Hymn to Apollo: The Ancient World and the Ballets Russes* (New York: Institute for the Study of the Ancient World at New York University; Princeton: Princeton University Press; 2019).

81 Nancy Van Norman Baer, "Design and Choreography: Cross-influences in the Theatrical Art of the Ballets Russes," in Baer, *Art of Enchantment*, 65.

82 Bellow, *Modernism on Stage*, 45.

83 Léon Bakst, in "Tout-Paris," "Bloc-Notes Parisien: Décors de Théâtre" (3 June 1911); AR, R012519 (volume 1). Quoted in Bellow, *Modernism on Stage*, 45.

84 The opening flute solo in Debussy's music manuscript (see p. 66), and the opening passage of Nijinsky's dance notation score for the same opening moment (see p. 72), correspond to the beginning of the ballet shown in fig. 27.

85 "An Explanation of Vaslav Nijinsky's System of Dance Notation," in Ann Hutchinson Guest and Claudia Jeschke, *Nijinsky's "Faune" Restored: A Study of Vaslav Nijinsky's 1915 Dance Score; "L'après-midi d'un faune" and His Dance Notation Method*, Language of Dance Series 3 (Binsted, UK: The Noverre Press, 1991), 46.

86 The sculptor August Rodin took Nijinsky's side in the public debate. Rodin was inspired by seeing the first performance of *Faune* to create a sculpture of Nijinsky in the role, held in the collection of the Metropolitan Museum of Art.

87 Lesure, *Debussy*, 286.

88 Nancy Van Norman Baer, *Bronislava Nijinska: A Dancer's Legacy*, exh. cat. (San Francisco: Fine Arts Museums of San Francisco, 1986), 26.

89 Bronislava Nijinska to Vera Krasovskaya describing the staging and choreography of *The Rite of Spring*, 11–12 December 1967. Typescript with handwritten corrections, titled: "1913. The Rite of spring." Bronislava Nijinska Collection, Library of Congress, Music Division, Washington, DC (hereafter, "Nijinska Collection"), Box 23, Folder 13.

90 Lesure, *Debussy*, 287.

91 Stephanie Jordan, *Moving Music: Dialogues with Music in Twentieth-Century Ballet* (London: Dance Books, 2000), 37–38.

92 Vaslav Nijinsky's four completed ballets were *L'Après-midi d'un Faune* (1912), *Jeux* (1913), *The Rite of Spring* (1913), and *Till Eulenspiegel*, choreographed to a score by Richard Strauss and premiered in the United States in 1916.

93 Igor Markevitch, "Préface pour l'édition de la notation chorégraphique de Nijinsky," in Françoise Stanciu-Reiss and Jean-Michel Pourvoyeur, *Écrits sur Nijinsky* (Paris: Éditions Chiron, 2008), 207. Quoted in Irene Brandenburg and Claudia Jeschke, *Tanz Schreiben: Artefakte, Hypertexte—und Nijinsky*, Tanz & Archiv: Forschungsreisen 10 (Munich: Epodium, 2023), 66. Translation from French by Robinson McClellan.

94 Nijinsky likely wrote this notation for *Faune* in early 1913 in Berlin or London (Nijinska, *Early Memoirs*, fig. 102).

95 While Nijinsky read music, he often relied on his excellent musical memory. Bronislava Nijinska recalled his ability to play complete pieces after hearing them only a few times. Bronislava Nijinska to Vera Krasovskaya describing the staging and choreography of *The Rite of Spring*, 1967. Nijinska Collection, Box 23, Folder 13.

96 Guest and Jeschke, *Nijinsky's "Faune" Restored*, 147–76.

97 Claudia Jeschke, "A Simple and Logical Means: Nijinsky, the Spirit of the Times, and *Faun*," in Ann Hutchinson Guest, Claudia Jeschke, and Philippe Néagu, *Afternoon of a Faun: Mallarmé, Debussy, Nijinsky*, ed. Jean-Michel Nectoux, trans. Maximilian Vos, exh. cat. (New York: Vendome Press, 1989), 110.

98 Claudia Jeschke, "Gedächtnistransfers, Spurensuchen—und Nijinsky," in Brandenburg and Jeschke, *Tanz Schreiben*, 71. Translation from the German provided by Jeschke.

99 Ibid., 70.

100 Nijinska, *Early Memoirs*, 301. Bronislava Nijinska was physically present and creatively active in every ballet featured in this exhibition and book, from *Firebird* to *Bolero*.

101 Quoted in Robert Craft, *Igor and Vera Stravinsky: A Photograph Album, 1921 to 1971* (London: Thames & Hudson, 1982), 12.

102 While Nijinska's *Early Memoirs* recounts parts of her own life, she frames it as her memories of her brother; she originally titled it *My Brother Vatsa*.

103 Baer, *Bronislava Nijinska*, 16.

104 Nijinska, *Early Memoirs*, 462.

105 Lynn Garafola, *La Nijinska: Choreographer of the Modern* (New York: Oxford University Press, 2022), 23–30. A manuscript in the Robert Owen Lehman Collection titled "III Fugato" may contain sketches of an arrangement Ravel drafted for Nijinsky of another popular Ballets Russes work, Fokine's 1910 *Carnaval* to music by Robert Schumann. Schumann's autograph manuscripts of *Carnaval* are held in the Morgan Library's music manuscripts collection.

106 Vaslav Nijinsky, *The Diary of Vaslav Nijinsky: Unexpurgated Edition*, ed. Joan Acocella, trans. Kyril FitzLyon (New York: Farrar, Straus & Giroux, 1999; repr. Urbana and Chicago: University of Illinois Press, 2006), xviii.

107 Many of Vaslav Nijinsky's drawings are held at the John Neumeier Foundation and appear in the exhibition catalogue *Tanz der Farben: Nijinskys Auge und die Abstraktion* (Hamburg: Hamburger Kunsthalle, 2009).

108 Nijinsky titled his manuscript *Feeling* (*Chuvstvo*), a mixture of letters, verse, and prose he structured in two parts, "On Life" and "On Death." He wrote it in just six weeks in four notebooks beginning in January 1919, up to the day he was institutionalized in March. For its conception and potential as a literary work, see Nicole Svobodny, *Nijinsky's Feeling Mind: The Dancer Writes, The Writer Dances* (New York: Lexington Books, 2023). The first 1936 and 1937 editions (fig. 32) were edited by Nijinsky's wife, Romola Nijinsky, who substantially cut, rearranged, and revised her husband's original work, deleting sexually explicit references to Diaghilev and unflattering ones to herself. The full unexpurgated text, edited by Joan Acocella, was published in 1999 (see n. 106).

109 Jeschke and Haitzinger, *Schwäne und Feuervögel*, 78. Also see Brandenburg and Jeschke, *Tanz Schreiben*.

110 Vaslav Nijinsky, Notebook no. 3 with notes on choreography, 1918. Museum of the Bolshoi Theatre. Courtesy of Elena Frolova, Ivan Strelkin, and Claudia Jeschke. The Nijinska Collection, Box 1, Folder 1, holds what appears to be a 1960 copy of one of Nijinsky's dance notation notebooks of 1917.

111 H.F.P., "Nijinsky Writing Book to Perpetuate His Art," *Musical America* (16 April 1916): 3. Quoted in Brandenburg and Jeschke, *Tanz Schreiben*, 66–67.

112 Dance notation systems used in the eighteenth and nineteenth centuries include Feuillet, Sténochorégraphie, and Stepanov. Benesh notation and Labanotation are among the main systems used today.

113 Wendy Lesser, "The Woman Who Was Written Out of the History of Dance," a *New York Times* review of Lynn Garafola's *La Nijinska*, 14 June 2022. See Anna Pakes, *Choreography Invisible* (2020), and Frédéric Pouillaude, *Unworking Choreography* (2017).

114 One can identify three phases in Nijinsky biography. First famous primarily as a dancer, his legacy as a choreographer was obscured thanks in part to the loss of his choreography for *Jeux* and *The Rite of Spring*, and the disparaging views of both Debussy and Stravinsky, which were widely received. His importance as a choreographer began to be recognized in the 1970s in biographies by Richard Buckle and Lincoln Kirstein, and in reconstructions of Nijinsky's original choreography for *The Rite of Spring*, staged in 1987 by Millicent Hodson and Kenneth Archer, and *L'Après-midi d'un Faune* in 1989, staged by Ann Hutchinson Guest and Claudia Jeschke (Jordan, *Moving Music*, 37). In recent decades his importance as a dance notator has emerged through the work of Guest, Jeschke, and others.

115 Baer, *Bronislava Nijinska*, 18.

116 Bronislava Nijinska, draft letter to Nijinsky, undated [Mar. 1919]. Quoted in Garafola, *La Nijinska*, 47–48.

117 Nijinska was inspired in this endeavor by Constructivist painter and theater designer Alexandra Exter. Garafola, *La Nijinska*, 39.

118 Bronislava Nijinska, treatise, "The School and Theater of Movement 1918," 19–21. Nijinska Collection, Box 22, Folder 9. Quoted in Garafola, *La Nijinska*, 40.

119 One of the few attempts at contact during this period, a letter Nijinska sent her brother in Switzerland in March 1919, has been lost. Garafola, *La Nijinska*, 47.

120 *Bronislava Nijinska—Svadebka Archives (2019–2023)*, 454. A digital book intended to make available, in an interactive form, the Bronislava Nijinska Collection of the Library of Congress concerning *Les Noces* (*Svadebka*). Designed by Dominique Brun, Ivan Chaumeille, and Sophie Jacotot. French translation from Russian by Mariia Nevzorova, texts collected and presented by Ivan Chaumeille. Subsidized by and available at the Centre National de la Danse in Pantin, France. Translation from French by Robinson McClellan.

121 Garafola, *La Nijinska*, 70.

122 Bronislava Nijinska's diary, 2 June 1921. Quoted in Garafola, *La Nijinska*, 73.

123 Translation via the Nijinska Collection, Box 47, Folder 1.

124 Nijinska appeared as the Chosen Maiden in Léonide Massine's 1920 production of *The Rite of Spring*, and, in a revival of her brother's *L'Après-midi d'un Faune* with a new backdrop by Pablo Picasso, she danced the (male) role of the Faun.

125 Igor Stravinsky's autograph manuscript of *Le Renard* is held in the Robert Owen Lehman Collection on deposit at the Morgan Library & Museum (see Garafola fig. 21).

126 Richard Taruskin, *Stravinsky and the Russian Traditions: A Biography of the Works through "Mavra,"* vol. 2 (Berkeley: University of California Press, 1996), 1323.

127 Alexander Pushkin, *Eugene Onegin: A Novel in Verse by Aleksandr Pushkin, Translated from the Russian, with a Commentary, by Vladimir Nabokov*, vol. 2 (New York: Pantheon Books, 1964), 162. The Morgan Library & Museum, PML 177155-58.

128 Drue Fergison, "Bringing *Les Noces* to the Stage," in Garafola and Baer, *The Ballets Russes and Its World*, 167–68.

129 Margarita Mazo, "Igor Stravinsky's *Les Noces*, the Rite of Passage," in *Les Noces (Svadebka)* (London: Chester Music, 2005), xi.

130 Announced in a 1915 issue of *Muzïka*, a Moscow music magazine. Taruskin, *Stravinsky and the Russian Traditions*, 1320.

131 Fergison, "Bringing *Les Noces* to the Stage," 170.

132 Mazo, in *Les Noces*, xv.

133 Igor Stravinsky and Robert Craft, *Expositions and Developments* (Berkeley: University of California Press, 1981), 118.

134 See Stephen Walsh, *Stravinsky: A Creative Spring: Russia and France, 1882–1934* (New York: Alfred A. Knopf, 1999), 273, and Taruskin, *Stravinsky and the Russian Traditions*, 1332. Igor Stravinsky's autograph manuscript of *Podblyudniye: Four Russian Peasant Songs* is held in the Morgan Library's Mary Flagler Cary Music Collection.

135 Stravinsky's 1919 version of *Les Noces* for solo voices, pianola, two cimbaloms, harmonium and percussion, including only the first two scenes, was premiered in a 1974 recording produced by John McClure and Robert Craft, with Orpheus Chamber Ensemble and the Gregg Smith Singers. Stravinsky's 1917 version was performed for the first time at Columbia University in 1973.

136 Jordan, *Stravinsky Dances*, 374.

137 Jordan, *Moving Music*, 328–29. Few of Stravinsky's piano rolls survive, and his sketches for pianola are rare; this manuscript, and one he made for *Petrouchka* in 1918 held at the Library of Congress, are among the few.

138 According to the dancer Serge Lifar. Jordan, *Stravinsky Dances*, 344.

139 John E. Bowlt, "From Studio to Stage: The Painters of the Ballets Russes," in Baer, *Art of Enchantment*, 52.

140 Mazo, in *Les Noces*, xii.

141 Fergison, "Bringing *Les Noces* to the Stage," 170.

142 In John Martin, "The Dance: Revival of Nijinska's 'Les Noces,'" *New York Times*, 3 May 1936, X7.

143 Bronislava Nijinska, "Creation of *Les Noces*," regarding the 1966 Royal Ballet performance of *Les Noces*, 6. Nijinska Collection, Box 7, Folder 10.

144 Translation noted in the Nijinska Collection with Stravinsky's letter to Nijinska, 27 March 1923. Box 82, Folder 6.

145 Nijinska, "Creation of *Les Noces*," 7.

146 Bronislava Nijinska, "Reflections about the Production of *Les Biches* and *Hamlet* in Markova-Dolin Ballets," trans. Lydia Lopokova, *Dancing Times*, February 1937, 617–18. Quoted in Garafola, *La Nijinska*, 135.

147 Nijinska, "Creation of *Les Noces*," 3.

148 Leonard Bernstein discussed this in *Les Noces*, a 1978 BBC Television documentary presented by John Drummond and directed by Robert Lockyer that includes a full performance of the work by the Royal Ballet. New York Public Library for the Performing Arts, *MGZIDVD 5-5528.

149 Fergison, "Bringing *Les Noces* to the Stage," 184.

150 In a program for the 1936 season June–September of Col. W. de Basil's Ballets Russes de Monte-Carlo. Adapted from an interview with Diaghilev published after the London premiere of the ballet ("'Les Noces.' M. Diaghileff Replies to the Critics," *The Observer*, 20 June 1926, 11).

151 Garafola, *La Nijinska*, 193.

152 Ibid., xviii.

153 The autograph manuscript of Stravinsky's *Ragtime* is held in the Robert Owen Lehman Collection on deposit at the Morgan Library & Museum.

154 In Jack Anderson, "The Fabulous Career of Bronislava Nijinska," *Dance Magazine*, August 1963, 40–46.

155 Manuscript draft by Bronislava Nijinska for a brochure for her School of Movement, 1924, [3]. Nijinska Collection, Box 65, Folder 5. French translation by Mariia Nevzorova in *Bronislava Nijinska—Svadebka Archives*, 458. Translation from French by Robinson McClellan.

156 Nijinska's ballet school in Kyiv had required study in music theory and dance notation. Garafola, *La Nijinska*, 47.

157 Claudia Jeschke, "*Les Noces*—Repetition: Variation: Transformation. Bronislawa Nijinska als Choreo-Graphin," in *Zur Ästhetik des Vorläufigen*, ed. Thomas Hochradner and Sarah Haslinger (Heidelberg: Universitätsverlag Winter, 2014), 105–19, at 115. Translation by Jeschke.

158 French translation by Mariia Nevzorova in *Bronislava Nijinska—Svadebka Archives*, 223. Translation from French by Robinson McClellan.

159 Jeschke, "*Les Noces*—Repetition: Variation: Transformation," 112, fig. 1.

160 Nijinska, "Creation of *Les Noces*," 6.

161 See Jordan, *Stravinsky Dances*, 356.

162 French translation by Mariia Nevzorova in *Bronislava Nijinska—Svadebka Archives*, 21. Translation from French by Robinson McClellan.

163 Garafola, *La Nijinska*, 3.

164 Nijinska Collection, Box 141, Folder 1, and Box 1, Folder 7.

165 Thomas, "Le peintre Bakst," 92.

166 Fokine, *Memoirs of a Ballet Master*, 137–38.

167 Maxime Girard, "Les Débuts de Mme Ida Rubinstein racontés par Léon Bakst," in the Théâtre du Vaudeville program for

L'Idiot, n.d., [1926]. Ida Rubinstein Collection, Library of Congress, Music Division, Washington, DC, Box 32, Folder 9.

168 Benois, "Origins of the Ballets Russes," 12.

169 Ibid., 12.

170 Scheijen, *Diaghilev*, 221.

171 *Collection des plus beaux numéros de "Comoedia illustré" et des programmes consacrés aux ballets et galas russes depuis le début à Paris, 1909–1921* (Paris: M. de Brunoff, [1922?]). The Morgan Library & Museum, Mary Flagler Cary Music Collection, PMC 428. The publisher's son, Jean Brunoff, is the author of *Babar the Elephant*, of which the Morgan Library holds a significant collection.

172 Walsh, *Debussy*, 222.

173 Nozière, *Ida Rubinstein*, 5. Nozière wrote two plays that Rubinstein performed in: *Imroulcaïs, le roi errant* (1919) and Dostoevsky's *L'Idiot* (1925). Though factually unreliable, Nozière's short biography is a colorful and telling evocation of Rubinstein's personality and era.

174 Ida Rubinstein, "Les aspects de la vie moderne: 'L'Art aux trois visages.' Conférence de Mme Ida Rubinstein." *Conferencia: Journal de l'Université des Annales* 19, no. 7 (15 March 1925): 328–42.

175 Elie Richard, "Mme Ida Rubinstein fait aux Éudiants [*sic*] une conférence sur la tragédie grecque," *Paris Midi*, 16 December 1924. In "Recueil factice d'écrits, conférences et interviews de Ida Rubinstein, 1913–1933." Bibliothèque Nationale de France, Paris, 8-RO-12743.

176 Expressed in his 1908 article, "Beseda o balete" (see p. 43).

177 Anna Winestein, "Partenaires dans l'Art: la collaboration entre Alexandre Benois et Ida Rubinstein," in *Ida Rubinstein: Une utopie de la synthèse des arts à l'épreuve de la scène*, ed. Pascal Lécroart (Besançon, France: Presses Universitaires de Franche-Comté 1097, 2008), 194.

178 Garafola, *La Nijinska*, 267.

179 Jacques Depaulis, *Ida Rubinstein: Une inconnue jadis célèbre* (Paris: Éditions Honoré Champion, 1995), 359.

180 Garafola, *La Nijinska*, 244.

181 Alexandre Benois, diary entries for 17, 22, 25 May, 10, 26 June, and 4, 6 July 1927. Quoted in Garafola, *La Nijinska*, 242–43. Four of Maurice Ravel's autograph manuscripts of *Le Tombeau de Couperin* are held in the Robert Owen Lehman Collection on deposit at the Morgan Library & Museum.

182 Benois's plans included a ballet on the music of J. S. Bach which became *The Marriage of Psyche and Cupid* (*Les Noces de Psyché et de l'Amour*), premiered in 1928 by Ida Rubinstein's company.

183 Benois, *Reminiscences*, 365–66.

184 Arbie Orenstein, *Ravel: Man and Musician* (New York: Columbia University Press, 1975), 8.

185 Maurice Ravel's autograph manuscripts of *L'Heure espagnole* and *Rapsodie espagnole* are held in the Robert Owen Lehman Collection on deposit at the Morgan Library & Museum.

186 Joaquin Nin, "Comment est né Boléro de Ravel," *La Revue musicale* 19 (December 1938): 211–13.

187 Dates inscribed by Ravel in his full score autograph manuscript of *Bolero*, held in the Lehman Collection (see pp. 106–7).

188 Orenstein, *Ravel*, 10.

189 Maurice Ravel's autograph manuscript of *Jeux d'eau* is held in the Robert Owen Lehman Collection on deposit at the Morgan Library & Museum.

190 Walsh, *Debussy*, 138–39.

191 Orenstein, *Ravel*, 10.

192 Maurice Ravel, "Factory Gives Composer Inspiration." Unsigned interview, *Evening Standard*, 24 February 1932. Quoted in Arbie Orenstein, ed., *A Ravel Reader: Correspondence, Articles, Interviews* (New York: Columbia University Press, 1990), 490.

193 Deborah Mawer, *The Ballets of Maurice Ravel: Creation and Interpretation* (Aldershot, UK: Ashgate, 2006), 221.

194 Émile Vuillermoz, "La musique: la semaine des mécènes," *Excelsior*, 26 November 1928. Bibliothèque nationale de France, Paris, Dossier d'artiste: Ida Rubinstein. Translation by Robinson McClellan.

195 Manuel Cornejo, ed., *L'Intégrale: Correspondance (1895–1936), écrits et entretiens* (Paris: Le Passeur, 2018), 1184–86. See Maurice Ravel to Georgette Marnold, 2 September 1928, Lettres à Jean et Georgette Marnold, 1908–1928, NAF 18719, Bibliothèque Nationale de France, Département des Manuscrits, donated by Georgette Marnold, 1975.

196 Ravel's pencil sketch for *Bolero* is held at the Bibliothèque Nationale de France, Paris, MS 21917.

197 Bronislava Nijinska, notebook, probably ca. 1930s. Nijinska Collection, Box 16, Folder 10. French translation by Mariia Nevzorova in *Bronislava Nijinska—Svadebka Archives*, 308. Translation from French by Robinson McClellan.

198 Garafola, *La Nijinska*, 252.

199 Bronislava Nijinska, notebook. Nijinska Collection, Box 16, Folder 10. French translation by Mariia Nevzorova in *Bronislava Nijinska—Svadebka Archives*, 647. Translation from French by Robinson McClellan.

200 Ibid., 653. The choreographer Dominique Brun has staged reconstructions of *Les Noces*, *Bolero*, and other ballets using Nijinska's choreographic notations, like these.

201 Baer, *Bronislava Nijinska*, 60.

202 Mawer, *Ballets of Maurice Ravel*, 230.

203 Louis Laloy, "Un beau spectacle de l'Opéra: Les ballets de Mme Ida Rubinstein," *Ère nouvelle*, 25 November 1928, 1. Quoted in Garafola, *La Nijinska*, 253.

204 Garafola, *La Nijinska*, 266.

205 In a letter on 23 November 1928 to the dancer Serge Lifar. Quoted in Scheijen, *Diaghilev*, 427.

206 François Dru and Quentin Hindley, eds., *Bolero*, Ravel Edition, vol. 1 (Linkebeek, Belgium: XXI Music Publishing, 2018), xxxii.

207 Natalia Goncharova also designed a production of *Firebird* in 1926 for Diaghilev (see Garafola's essay, fig. 2).

208 Francis Poulenc, *Moi et mes amis* (Paris: Éditions La Palatine, 1963), 179.

209 *La Valse* had received its ballet premiere at the Flemish Opera in 1926.

210 Diaghilev, Stravinsky, and others shared a lifelong love of Tchaikovsky's music, which wound its way through the history of the Ballets Russes, including productions of *Swan Lake* in 1911 and *The Sleeping Princess* in 1921. The Morgan Library & Museum holds Diaghilev's heavily revised copy of *Swan Lake*, a mix of printed score and manuscript pages he and his collaborators stitched together.

211 Igor Stravinsky's autograph manuscript of *Perséphone* is held in the Mary Flagler Cary Music Collection at the Morgan Library & Museum, gift of Robert Owen Lehman.

212 Arthur Honegger's autograph manuscript of *Jeanne d'Arc au Bûcher* is held at the Morgan Library & Museum, gift of Robert Owen Lehman.

213 Jordan, *Stravinsky Dances*, 293.

214 Ravel's autograph manuscript sketches, likely for the unrealized ballet *Morgiane*, are held in the Robert Owen Lehman Collection on deposit at the Morgan Library & Museum. They may be the last musical notations Ravel made before his death in 1937. See Cornejo, *L'Intégrale*, 1307.

215 The obituary by Gérard Bauër is referred to in René Dumesnil, "Souvenirs sur Ida Rubinstein," *Le Monde*, 26 October 1960.

"L'APRES MIDI D'UN FA..
(NIJINSKY)

4me Année.   No 16
15 Mai 1912
Numéro Exceptionnel
60 Pages

PRIX
1 fr. 50

7me Saison

Checklist of the Exhibition

Léon Bakst (1866–1924), Set design for bedroom scene for *Schéhérazade*, [1910]. Gouache on paper; 24¾ × 29⅛ in. (63 × 74 cm). Boris Stavrovski Collection, New York.

p. 38

Flyer for Serge Diaghilev's 1910 Saison Russe featuring ballet "créations" (premieres) including *Schéhérazade* and *Firebird* (*L'Oiseau de Feu*). 9 × 6⅛ in. (22.9 × 15.4 cm). The Morgan Library & Museum, New York, James Fuld Collection.

p. 39

Serge Diaghilev (1872–1929), Autograph letter to an unidentified recipient, St. Petersburg, 31 October 1900. *Mir iskusstva* letterhead with illustration by Léon Bakst (1866–1924). The Morgan Library & Museum, New York, James Fuld Collection.

p. 42

Valentin Serov (1865–1911), Portrait of Michel Fokine. Lithograph after the 1909 drawing; 19 × 15 in. (48.3 × 38.1 cm). Private collection, New York.

p. 45, reproduced in "*Comoedia illustré.*"

Abraham Walkowitz (1878–1965), Isadora Duncan, n.d. Pen and pencil on paper; 19 × 16 in. (48.3 × 40.6 cm). Private collection, New York.

Jacques-Émile Blanche (1861–1942), Ida Rubinstein as Zobéide in *Schéhérazade*, ca. 1910. Oil on canvas; 35 × 46 in. (89.5 × 116.5 cm). Harvard Theatre Collection, Houghton Library, Howard D. Rothschild Collection; pfMS Thr 414.4 (43).

p. 47

Léon Bakst (1866–1924), Design for the ballet *Les Orientales*, 1910. Watercolor and graphite on paper; 14¹⁵⁄₁₆ × 17⅜ in. (37.9 × 44.1 cm). The Morgan Library & Museum, New York, gift of Mrs. Donald M. Oenslager, 1982; 1982.75:678.

Ivan Bilibin (1876–1942), Illustration from *Skazka ob Ivane-tsareviche, Zhar-ptitse i o serom volke* [Tale of Ivan-Tsarevich, the Firebird, and the Grey Wolf], from the series "Skazki" [Folk tales] by Alexander Afanasyev, pp. 2–3 (St. Petersburg: Ekspeditsiya zagotovleniya gosudarstvennikh bumag, 1901). The Morgan Library & Museum, New York, purchased on the Elisabeth Ball Fund, 1992; PML 86045.

p. 48

Igor Stravinsky (1882–1971), "Adagio / Supplication of the Firebird" from *Firebird*, autograph manuscript, piano, extensive revisions, pp. 12–13, [1910], inscribed 1918. The Morgan Library & Museum, New York, Robert Owen Lehman Collection, on deposit.

p. 48

Igor Stravinsky, around the time he met Serge Diaghilev and Michel Fokine. Silver print postcard; 5½ × 3½ in. (14 × 9.1 cm). Fabrice Herrault Collection.

p. 18

Léon Bakst (1866–1924), Costume design for *Firebird*, 1910. Pencil, watercolor, and gouache, heightened with gold on paper; 13¾ × 8⅝ in. (35 × 22 cm). Private collection.

p. 50

Léon Bakst (1866–1924), Costume design for *Firebird*, 1913. Metallic paint, gouache, watercolor, and pencil on paper on board; 26½ × 19¼ in. (67.3 × 48.9 cm). The Museum of Modern Art, New York, the Joan and Lester Avnet Collection; 4.1978.

p. 51

Léon Bakst (1866–1924), Poster design for *Firebird*, "Firebird and the Prince (Tsarevitch)," 1915. Watercolor, pencil, and illustration board; 19¼ × 14 in. (49 × 33 cm). Harvard Theatre Collection, Houghton Library, Howard D. Rothschild Collection; pfMS Thr 414.4 (13).

p. 52

← Léon Bakst (1866–1924), Costume illustration for Vaslav Nijinsky as the Faun in *L'Après-midi d'un Faune* (*Afternoon of a Faun*), 1912. Reproduced in *Collection des plus beaux numéros de "Comoedia illustré" et des programmes consacrés aux ballets et galas russes depuis le début à Paris, 1909–1921*. The Morgan Library & Museum, New York, Mary Flagler Cary Music Collection.

Tamara Karsavina and Michel Fokine in *Firebird*, 1910. Photograph; 7¾ × 5 in. (19 × 12.7 cm). Library of Congress, Bronislava Nijinska Collection; Box 61, Folder 26.
 p. 53

Igor Stravinsky (1882–1971), *Firebird*, orchestral score, copyist manuscript likely created by Stravinsky's first wife, Catherine, pp. 22–23, [1910]. Contains conductor's markings and revisions by the composer. From the library of Serge Diaghilev. The Morgan Library & Museum, New York, Mary Flagler Cary Music Collection; Cary 55.

Igor Stravinsky (1882–1971), *Firebird*, orchestral parts, copyist manuscript, annotated by musicians, ca. 1910–29. From the library of Serge Diaghilev. The Morgan Library & Museum, New York, Mary Flagler Cary Music Collection; PMC 88–89.
 p. 18

Igor Stravinsky (1882–1971), *Firebird*, first edition of the score, numerous annotations and revisions in the composer's hand, pp. 70–[71] (Moscow: P. Jurgenson, [n.d.]). The Morgan Library & Museum, New York, Robert Owen Lehman Collection, on deposit.
 p. 55

Michel Fokine (1880–1942), *Against the Tide: Memoirs of a Ballet Master*, introduction by Yuri Slonimsky (Leningrad: Iskusstvo, 1962). Choreographic notations for *Firebird*, pp. [260–61]. Private collection, New York.
 p. 56

Léon Bakst (1866–1924), Design for the ballet *Narcisse* and insert for the *Petrouchka* premiere. Reproduced in the *Comoedia illustré* souvenir program for the 6–17 June 1911 Ballets Russes season at the Théâtre du Châtelet, Paris. The Morgan Library & Museum, New York, James Fuld Collection.

Igor Stravinsky (1882–1971), *Petrouchka*, autograph manuscript, full score, pp. 70–71, 26 May 1911. The Morgan Library & Museum, New York, Robert Owen Lehman Collection, on deposit.
 p. 57

Igor Stravinsky (1882–1971), *Three Movements from Petrouchka*, autograph manuscript, piano, p. 1, 4 September 1921. The Morgan Library & Museum, New York, Robert Owen Lehman Collection, on deposit.

Alexandre Benois (1870–1960), Set design for the Butter Week Fair for *Petrouchka*, scenes 1 and 4, 1911. Graphite, tempera, and watercolor on paper; 17⅝ × 24¼ in. (45 × 62 cm). Wadsworth Atheneum, Hartford; 1933.402.
 p. 58

Alexandre Benois (1870–1960), Costume design for a moujik in *Petrouchka*, n.d. Gouache and black ink with graphite on paper; 12¼ × 9⅛ in. (31.1 × 23 cm). The Morgan Library & Museum, New York, Joseph F. McCrindle Collection; 2009.23.

Alexandre Benois (1870–1960), Costume design "No. 40" for *Petrouchka*, n.d. Watercolor and pen on paper; 12¼ × 9¼ in. (31.1 × 23.5 cm). Private collection.

Alexandre Benois (1870–1960), Costume design for the Crow in *Petrouchka*, 1956. Watercolor and pen on paper; 12 × 8¾ in. (30.5 × 22.2 cm). Private collection.

Dover Street Studios (London, active ca. 1906–ca. 1912), Vaslav Nijinsky as Petrouchka, [1911], no. 2054. Photograph; 14 × 10⅜ in. (35.6 × 26.3 cm). Library of Congress, Ida Rubinstein Collection; Box 31, Folder 6.
 p. 59

Alexandre Benois (1870–1960), "Arap," in *Azbuka v kartinakh* [Alphabet in Pictures] (Saint Petersburg: Expedition of State Papers, 1904). The Morgan Library & Museum, New York, purchased on the Elisabeth Ball Fund, 1992; PML 86042.
 p. 60

Igor Stravinsky "Author," Vaslav Nijinsky "Interpreter," Alexander Orlov as the Moor in *Petrouchka*, 1911. Reproduced in *Collection des plus beaux numéros de "Comoedia illustré" et des programmes consacrés aux ballets et galas russes depuis le début à Paris, 1909–1921* (Paris: M. de Brunoff, [1922?]). The Morgan Library & Museum, New York, Mary Flagler Cary Music Collection; PMC 428.
 p. 61

Léon Bakst (1866–1924), Illustration for Ida Rubinstein as St. Sebastian in *The Martyrdom of St. Sebastian*; composer Claude Debussy, poet Gabriele D'Annunzio, artist Léon Bakst. Reproduced in *Comoedia illustré: numéro spécial*, vol. 3, no. 17, 1 June 1911. The Morgan Library & Museum, New York, Mary Flagler Cary Music Collection, purchased 2022; PMC 2818.

> p. 62

Claude Debussy (1862–1918), Letter to D. E. Inghelbrecht regarding Ida Rubinstein and *The Martyrdom of St. Sebastian*, 22 May 1912. The Morgan Library Music Collection, gift of Margaret G. Cobb, 2004.

Léon Bakst (1866–1924), *Daphnis and Chloë*, Costume design for Tamara Karsavina as Chloë, 1912. Graphite and tempera on paper; 11⅛ × 17¹¹⁄₁₆ in. (28.3 × 44.9 cm). Wadsworth Atheneum, Hartford; 1933.392.

> p. 22

Jean Cocteau (1889–1963), *Serge Diaghilev and Vaslav Nijinsky*. Pen on paper, 1961 version of a 1913 original; 10½ × 8⅛ in. (26.8 × 20.8 cm). The New York Public Library, Jerome Robbins Dance Division; *MGZGA Coc J Dya 1.

> p. 64

Serge Diaghilev (1872–1929), "Black Exercise Book," pp. 14–15, 1910. The New York Public Library, Jerome Robbins Dance Division; *MGZMB-Res. 72-92.

Stéphane Mallarmé (1842–1898), *L'Après-midi d'un faune*, with illustrations by Édouard Manet, title page (Paris: Alphonse Derenne, 1876). The Morgan Library & Museum, New York, bequest of Gordon N. Ray, 1987; PML 140627.

Claude Debussy (1862–1918), *Prélude à l'après-midi d'un faune*, autograph manuscript, short score (particell), p. 1, 1894. The Morgan Library & Museum, New York, Robert Owen Lehman Collection, on deposit.

> pp. 66–67

Bronislava Nijinska (1891–1972), Léon Bakst in Karlsbad (Karlovy Vary), 1910. Photograph; 5 × 7¼ in. (12.7 × 18.4 cm). Library of Congress, Bronislava Nijinska Collection; Box 60, Folder 23.

> p. 68

Léon Bakst (1866–1924), Sketchbook, likely from a visit to Greece and Crete, p. 10, 1907(?). Pencil and watercolor on paper; 8 × 5⅛ in. (20.3 × 13 cm). The New York Public Library, Jerome Robbins Dance Division; (S) *MGZGV-Res.

> p. 68

Léon Bakst (1866–1924), Costume design for a nymph in *L'Après-midi d'un Faune* (*Afternoon of a Faun*), 1912. Watercolor, pencil, and gold paint on paper; 17¼ × 14¼ in. (44 × 36 cm). Harvard Theatre Collection, Houghton Library, Stravinsky-Diaghilev Foundation Collection; pfMS Thr 495 (261).

> p. 69

Adolf de Meyer (1868–1946), *L'Après-midi d'un Faune*, 1912. Hand-enhanced photographs, nos. 2000, 2001, 2003, 2005, 2006, 2007, 2014; various dimensions. The New York Public Library, Jerome Robbins Dance Division; *MGZEC 84-819, Box 1.

> p. 70

Auguste Rodin (1840–1917), Nijinsky in *Afternoon of a Faun*, modeled 1912, cast 1959. Bronze, marble base; 6¾ × 2⅞ × 2⅝ in. (17.1 × 7.3 × 6.7 cm). The Metropolitan Museum of Art, New York, gift in honor of B. Gerald Cantor; 1991.446.

Vaslav Nijinsky (1890–1950), *L'Après-midi d'un Faune*, choreographic notation, [1913]. Library of Congress, Bronislava Nijinska Collection; Box 29, Folder 13.

> p. 73

Claude Debussy (1862–1918), Sketchbook, autograph manuscript with the composer's pencil, ca. 1908–10. Containing a sketch possibly for the unrealized 1910 ballet *Masques et Bergamasques*. The Morgan Library & Museum, New York, Robert Owen Lehman Collection, on deposit.

Claude Debussy (1862–1918), *Jeux*, autograph manuscript, "préparation orchestrale" (pre-orchestral draft), p. 1, April 1913. The Morgan Library & Museum, New York, Robert Owen Lehman Collection, on deposit.

> p. 20

Valentine Gross (1887–1968), Drawings of Vaslav Nijinsky's choreography for *Jeux*, 1913, reproduced in *Comoedia illustré*, 15 June 1913. Fabrice Herrault Collection.

p. 21

Igor Stravinsky (1882–1971), *The Rite of Spring / Le Sacre du Printemps: Sketches, 1911–1913; Facsimile Reproductions from the Autographs*, pp. 96–[97] ([London]: Boosey & Hawkes, 1969). The Morgan Library & Museum, New York, Mary Flagler Cary Music Collection; PMC 2820.

p. 19

Nicholas Roerich (1874–1947), Illustration of costumes from *The Rite of Spring* (*Le Sacre du Printemps*), n.d. Watercolor and pencil; 9½ × 12¼ in. (24 × 31 cm). Harvard Theatre Collection, Houghton Library, Howard D. Rothschild Collection, bequest, 1989; pf MS Thr 414.4 (119).

Female dancers on stage in Nijinsky's original production of *The Rite of Spring* (*Le Sacre du Printemps*), [1913]. Photograph; 3¼ x 5 in. (8.2 × 12.7 cm). The New York Public Library, Jerome Robbins Dance Division; *MGZEA Rite of spring (Nijinsky).

Male dancers on stage in Nijinsky's original production of *The Rite of Spring* (*Le Sacre du Printemps*), [1913]. Photograph; 3¼ x 5 in. (8.2 × 12.7 cm). The New York Public Library, Jerome Robbins Dance Division; *MGZEA Rite of spring (Nijinsky).

Igor Stravinsky (1882–1971), "Danse sacrale" from *The Rite of Spring* (*Le Sacre du Printemps*), autograph manuscript, pp. [1]–2, 1947. Private collection.

Bronislava Nijinska (1891–1972), *The Rite of Spring* (*Le Sacre du Printemps*), drawing and description of collaboration between Stravinsky, Roerich, and Nijinsky, 1960s. Pencil on paper; 8 × 9 in. (20.3 × 22.9 cm). Library of Congress, Bronislava Nijinska Collection; Box 10, Folder 10.

Bronislava Nijinska (1891–1972) as the Street Dancer in *Petrouchka*, 1911. Reproduced in program for Diaghilev's eighth season in Paris, 21 June 1913. The Morgan Library & Museum, New York, James Fuld Collection.

p. 74

Poster for 1914 Saison Nijinsky, London, "The famous premier danseur/supported by Mlle. Nijinska." 19⅞ × 12⁹⁄₁₆ in. (50.5 × 31.9 cm). Library of Congress, Bronislava Nijinska Collection; Box 161, Folder 5.

p. 74

Vaslav Nijinsky and Maurice Ravel at Ravel's apartment, [1914]. Photograph; 8 × 10¾ in. (20.3 × 27.3 cm). Library of Congress, Bronislava Nijinska Collection; Box 29, Folder 13.

Vaslav Nijinsky (1890–1950), Notebook containing dance notation (pencil) and draft for the *Diary* (pen), pp. 122–23, 1918–19. Pen and pencil on paper. The New York Public Library, Jerome Robbins Dance Division; *MGZMB-Res. 94-2666.

pp. 78–79

Vaslav Nijinsky (1890–1950), *Diary*. (London: Victor Gollancz, 1937). Illustrated with drawings by Nijinsky, 1917–19. p. 176 and facing plate with reproduction of Nijinsky's portrait of Serge Diaghilev, 1919. The Morgan Library & Museum, New York, Mary Flagler Cary Music Collection, purchased 2022; PMC 2822.

p. 76

Vaslav Nijinsky (1890–1950), *Mask of God*, ca. 1919. Ink and gouache on paper; 10 × 8⅛ in. (25.5 × 20.7 cm). The New York Public Library, Jerome Robbins Dance Division; *MGZGB Nij V Mas 2.

Vadym Meller (1884–1962), Costume illustration for Bronislava Nijinska in *Fear*, Kyiv, 1919. Opaque water-based media (likely gouache) on paper; 24½ × 17 in. (62.2 × 43.2 cm). Library of Congress, Bronislava Nijinska Collection.

Bronislava Nijinska (1891–1972), Choreographic drawings, Kyiv, 1919. Pen on paper; 13 × 11 in. (33 × 27.9 cm) overall. Library of Congress, Bronislava Nijinska Collection; Box 145, Folder 13.

p. 81

Bronislava Nijinska (1891–1972), Self-portrait, 1921. Pencil on paper; 6½ × 7 in. (16.5 × 17.8 cm). Library of Congress, Bronislava Nijinska Collection; Box 47, Folder 1.

p. 82

Bronislava Nijinska in 1921 after leaving Kyiv. Photograph; 7 × 4½ in. (17.8 × 11.4 cm). Library of Congress, Bronislava Nijinska Collection; Box 48, Folder 1.

p. 82

"Les Ballets Russes à Mogador" program, [Paris], June 1922. The Morgan Library & Museum, New York, James Fuld Collection.

p. 83

Mikhail Larionov (1881–1964), Drawing of Serge Diaghilev, Igor Stravinsky, and Sergey Prokofiev, 1921. Pencil on paper; 17 × 13⅛ in. (43.2 × 33.3 cm). Harvard Theatre Collection, Houghton Library, Howard D. Rothschild Collection; pfMS Thr 414.4 (85).

p. 25

Igor Stravinsky (1882–1971), *Les Noces*, autograph manuscript, first draft in short score (particell) of the first tableau (to rehearsal [16] in the published score), versions 1–3, [1914–15]. Vellum cover hand-painted by Stravinsky. The Morgan Library & Museum, New York, Robert Owen Lehman Collection, on deposit.

p. 84

Igor Stravinsky (1882–1971), *Les Noces*, autograph manuscript, two pages of full-score instrumental sketches for the third tableau, [1914–15]. The Morgan Library & Museum, New York, Robert Owen Lehman Collection, on deposit.

p. 86

Pablo Picasso (1881–1973), *Portrait of Igor Stravinsky*, Rome, 1917. Graphite on cream wove paper; 10⅝ × 7⅞ in. (27 × 20 cm). Private collection.

p. 85

Natalia Goncharova (1881–1962), Curtain design for *Les Noces*, 1915. Opaque watercolor over graphite; 18½ × 27¾ in. (45.7 × 55.9 cm). Philadelphia Museum of Art; 1941-79-96.

p. 89

Natalia Goncharova (1881–1962), *Self-Portrait*, ca. 1907. Oil on canvas mounted on board; 22 × 18 in. (55.9 × 45.7 cm). Mead Art Museum, Amherst College, gift of Thomas P. Whitney; AC 2001.11.

p. 88

Igor Stravinsky (1882–1971), *Les Noces*, autograph manuscript, drafts for pianola arrangement, ca. 1919. The Morgan Library & Museum, New York, Mary Flagler Cary Music Collection, purchased with the special assistance of the Ann and Gordon Getty Foundation; Cary 567.

p. 87

Natalia Goncharova (1881–1962), Sketch for the stage design for *Les Noces*, 1923. Pen, brush, and ink on tracing paper; 13 × 17 in. (33 × 43.2 cm). The New York Public Library, Jerome Robbins Dance Division; *MGZGB Gon N Noc 1.

p. 90

Natalia Goncharova (1881–1962), Drawing of women in Nijinska's choreographic braid motif for *Les Noces*, 1923. Pen and ink on tracing paper mounted on paper; 21⅝ × 17⅝ in. (54.9 × 44.7 cm). Harvard Theatre Collection, Houghton Library, Howard D. Rothschild Collection; pfMS Thr 414.4 (61).

p. 91

Dancers on stage in *Les Noces*, 1923. Photograph; 5 × 8 in. (12.7 × 20.3 cm). Library of Congress, Bronislava Nijinska Collection; Box 42, Folder 6.

p. 91

Igor Stravinsky (1882–1971), Letter to Bronislava Nijinska regarding *Les Noces*, 27 March 1923. Library of Congress, Bronislava Nijinska Collection; Box 82, Folder 6.

p. 92

Pablo Picasso (1881–1973), *Portrait of Igor Stravinsky*, 31 December 1920. Pencil on paper; 13⅝ × 9½ in. (34.5 × 24.1 cm). Private collection.

p. 29

Alexey Brodovitch (1898–1971), *Ballet*, 104 photographs and text by Edwin Denby (New York: J.J. Augustin, [ca. 1945]). Photographs of *Les Noces* on stage, pp. 96–97, 1936. The Morgan Library & Museum, New York, gift, Family of Carter Burden; PML 175357.

Bronislava Nijinska rehearsing *Les Noces* in Monte Carlo, 1923. Photograph; 5 × 8 in. (12.7 × 20.3 cm). Library of Congress, Bronislava Nijinska Collection; Box 42, Folder 6.

p. 93

Bronislava Nijinska (1891–1972), Choreographic drawings for the first tableau of *Les Noces*: frontal elevation views of dancers, 1923. Pen on paper; 5¼ × 8¼ in. (13.3 × 21 cm). Library of Congress, Bronislava Nijinska Collection; Box 8, Folder 1.

p. 93

Bronislava Nijinska (1891–1972), Choreographic notes for the fourth tableau of *Les Noces*, 1923. Library of Congress, Bronislava Nijinska Collection; Box 8, Folder 1, Leaves 5v, 8r.

p. 94

Bronislava Nijinska (1891–1972), Choreographic drawings for *Les Noces*: frontal elevation views of dancers for the fourth tableau, ca. 1923. Pen on paper; 9¼ × 5 in. (23.5 × 12.7 cm). Library of Congress, Bronislava Nijinska Collection; Box 8, Folder 1.

p. 94

Bronislava Nijinska rehearsing the fourth tableau of *Les Noces* for the 1966 Royal Ballet production. Photograph; approx. 10 × 7½ in. (25.4 × 19.1 cm). Library of Congress, Bronislava Nijinska Collection; Box 9, Folder 1.

p. 95

Bronislava Nijinska as the Hostess in *Les Biches*, 1924. Photograph; 10 × 7 in. (25.4 × 17.8 cm). Library of Congress, Bronislava Nijinska Collection; Box 1, Folder 17.

p. 33

Dancers on stage in *Les Biches*, showing the backcloth by the ballet's designer, Marie Laurencin (1883–1956). Photograph; 6¼ × 8¾ in. (15.9 × 22.2 cm). Library of Congress, Bronislava Nijinska Collection; Box 1, Folder 17.

Francis Poulenc (1899–1963), *Les Biches*, autograph manuscript, choral score, title page and p. 2, 1923. The Morgan Library & Museum, New York, Mary Flagler Cary Music Collection, purchased 2020; Cary 721.2.

Pablo Picasso (1881–1973), *Deux Danseurs* (*Two Dancers*), 1925. Pen and black ink on tan wove paper; 13⅞ × 9⅞ in. (35.2 × 25.1 cm). The Morgan Library & Museum, New York, gift of Richard and Mary L. Gray; 2023.78.

Léon Bakst (1866–1924), *Mme Ida Rubinstein*, 1917. Watercolor, gouache, and graphite on paper, mounted on canvas; 50½ × 27¼ in. (128.3 × 69.2 cm). The Metropolitan Museum of Art, New York, the Chester Dale Collection, 1962; 64.97.1.

p. 103

Alexandre Benois (1870–1960), Costume design for Minerva in *Les Noces de Psyché et de l'Amour* (*The Marriage of Psyche and Cupid*), [1928]. Watercolor and pen on paper; 14½ × 10 in. (36.8 × 25.4 cm). Private collection.

Alexandre Benois (1870–1960), Costume design for the Poet in *La Bien-Aimée* (*The Beloved*), [1928]. Watercolor and pen on paper; 14½ × 10 in. (36.8 × 25.4 cm). Private collection.

Elliott & Fry (London, act. 1863–1962), Portrait of Maurice Ravel, inscribed to Louise Alvar, 23 October 1928, shortly after completing *Bolero*. Photograph; plate: 6½ × 4⅜ in. (16.4 × 11.1 cm); sheet: 11 × 8 in. (28 × 20.4 cm). The Morgan Library & Museum, New York, bequest of Charles Alvar Harding, 2001; M100.2.

p. 105

Maurice Ravel (1875–1937), *Bolero*, autograph manuscript, full score, p. 1, 1928. Dedication "to Ida Rubinstein." The Morgan Library & Museum, New York, Robert Owen Lehman Collection, on deposit.

pp. 106–7

Bronislava Nijinska (1891–1972), Notebook containing choreographic notes and drawings for *Bolero*, p. 1, [1928]. Library of Congress, Bronislava Nijinska Collection; Box 3, Folder 15.

p. 108

Bolero in rehearsal, 1928. Studio des Champs-Élysées, Paris. At center: Anatole Viltzak, Ida Rubinstein's co-lead. Photograph; 5⅞ × 8⁹⁄₁₆ in. (15 × 21.7 cm). Library of Congress, Bronislava Nijinska Collection; Box 3, Folder 9.

p. 110

Alexandre Benois (1870–1960), Costume design for the Matador in *Bolero*, 1928. Watercolor, pen, and pencil; 12⅝ × 9½ in. (32 × 24.1 cm). The New York Public Library, Jerome Robbins Dance Division; *MGZGA Ben A Bol 1.

p. 111

"Costumbres Andaluzas." Postcard, n.d. 5⅜ ×
3½ in. (13.7 × 8.9 cm). Library of Congress,
Bronislava Nijinska Collection; Box 59, Folder 2.
    p. 108

Ida Rubinstein with cast on stage in *Bolero*, 1928.
Photograph; 8½ × 11½ in. (21.6 × 29.2 cm).
Library of Congress, Bronislava Nijinska Collection;
Box 3, Folder 9.
    p. 109

Ida Rubinstein in costume for *Bolero* (with black
cat). Photograph; 8¾ × 6¼ in. (22.2 × 15.9 cm).
Library of Congress, Ida Rubinstein Collection;
Box 12, Folder 2.

Maurice Ravel (1875–1937), *La Valse*, autograph
manuscript, two pianos, cover page inscription,
[1920]. The Morgan Library & Museum, New York,
Robert Owen Lehman Collection, on deposit.

Maurice Ravel (1875–1937), *La Valse*, autograph
manuscript, solo piano, pp. 14–15, 1920. The
Morgan Library & Museum, New York, Mary Flagler
Cary Music Collection, gift of Robert Owen
Lehman; Cary 512.
    p. 112

Bronislava Nijinska (1891–1972), Sketch for
La Valse showing the stage with dancers' positions,
1929. Pen on paper; 7 × 5 in. (17.8 × 12.7 cm).
Library of Congress, Bronislava Nijinska Collection;
Box 21, Folder 16.
    p. 113

Alexandre Benois (1870–1960), Set design for
La Valse with conductor and dancing couples,
1930. Watercolor and pencil on paper; 13¾ × 20¼ in.
(30 × 49.5 cm). Harvard Theatre Collection,
Houghton Library; HTC 25,515 Designs.
    p. 112

Igor Stravinsky (1882–1971), *Le Baiser de la Fée*
(*The Fairy's Kiss*), autograph manuscript, piano,
title page and p. 1, 1928. The Morgan Library &
Museum, New York, Robert Owen Lehman
Collection, on deposit.

Bronislava Nijinska (1891–1972), *Le Baiser de la Fée*
(*The Fairy's Kiss*), printed score (Berlin: Russischer
Musikverlag, 1928) with choreographic notations,
p. 1, 1928. Library of Congress, Bronislava Nijinska
Collection; Box 141, Folder 1.

Program for Les Ballets de Madame Ida Rubinstein.
Académie Nationale de Musique et de Danse,
May 1929. Library of Congress, Ida Rubinstein
Collection; Box 32, Folder 11.
    p. 115

Ida Rubinstein (1883–1960), Autograph letter to
an unidentified friend, [Paris], 6 December 1934.
The Morgan Library & Museum, New York, James
Fuld Collection.

Flyer for Les Ballets de Madame Ida Rubinstein,
featuring *Bolero*, *La Valse*, *Perséphone*, etc., 1934.
10 × 5⅞ in. (25.4 × 14.9 cm). Library of Congress,
Ida Rubinstein Collection; Box 32, Folder 19.
    p. 115

Ballet and Related Music Manuscripts in the Robert Owen Lehman and Morgan Library Collections

The following list includes the autograph music manuscripts, and print editions with annotations in the composer's hand, held in the Robert Owen Lehman Collection on deposit and in the Morgan Library's Mary Flagler Cary and James Fuld collections, for ballets and related stage works produced by Serge Diaghilev and Ida Rubinstein between 1910 and 1938. Also included are additional music manuscripts for French and Russian ballets produced during the same period. All works are held at the Morgan Library & Museum, New York.

Claude Debussy (1862–1918)

Jeux. Commissioned and produced by Diaghilev's Ballets Russes, 1913.
— autograph manuscript, "préparation orchestrale" (pre-orchestral draft), April 1913. Robert Owen Lehman Collection, on deposit. p. 20

Prélude à l'après-midi d'un faune. Produced as a ballet by Diaghilev's Ballets Russes, 1912.
— autograph manuscript, short score (particell), 1894. Robert Owen Lehman Collection, on deposit. pp. 66–67
— autograph manuscript, two-piano version, 1895. Robert Owen Lehman Collection, on deposit.
— Paris: E. Fromont, [1894–95?]. From the library of Serge Diaghilev. Mary Flagler Cary Music Collection. Annotated conducting score; PMC 82. Orchestral parts; PMC 84.

Sketchbook
— autograph manuscript, containing a sketch possibly for the unrealized 1910 Diaghilev ballet *Masques et Bergamasques*. Robert Owen Lehman Collection, on deposit.

Maurice Ravel (1875–1937)

Bolero. Commissioned and produced by Les Ballets de Madame Ida Rubinstein, 1928.
— autograph manuscript, full score, 1928. Dedication on first page "to Ida Rubinstein." Robert Owen Lehman Collection, on deposit. pp. 106–7

L'Enfant et les Sortilèges. Opera-ballet produced with "Artists of the Ballets Russes" and George Balanchine, choreographer, 1925.
— autograph manuscript, vocal score, 1920–25. Robert Owen Lehman Collection, on deposit.

Morgiane. Commissioned by Ida Rubinstein; score never completed.
— autograph manuscript, sketches for an unrealized ballet, [1930s]. Robert Owen Lehman Collection, on deposit.

Pavane de la Belle au Bois Dormant (*Sleeping Beauty*) from *Ma Mère l'Oye* (*Mother Goose*). Produced as a ballet by Jacques Rouché, 1912.
— autograph manuscript, piano four hands, 1908. Robert Owen Lehman Collection, on deposit.

Le Tombeau de Couperin. Produced as a ballet by the Ballets Suédois, Rolf de Maré, 1920.
— autograph manuscript, full score, 1919. Robert Owen Lehman Collection, on deposit.
— autograph manuscript, draft of the orchestral version, [1919?]. Robert Owen Lehman Collection, on deposit.
— autograph manuscript, sketches and drafts of the original piano version, [1919]. Robert Owen Lehman Collection, on deposit.
— "Oiseaux Tristes" from *Miroirs* [1905], with sketch for the Fugue from *Le Tombeau de Couperin*. Mary Flagler Cary Music Collection; Cary 297.

La Valse. Composed for Diaghilev's Ballets Russes, 1920; produced by Les Ballets de Madame Ida Rubinstein, 1929.
— autograph manuscript, full score, 1920. Robert Owen Lehman Collection, on deposit.
— autograph working manuscript for two-piano arrangement, [1920?]. Robert Owen Lehman Collection, on deposit.
— autograph manuscript, solo piano, 1920. Mary Flagler Cary Music Collection, gift of Robert Owen Lehman; Cary 512. p. 112

Igor Stravinsky (1882–1971)

Le Baiser de la Fée (*The Fairy's Kiss*).
Commissioned and produced by Les Ballets de
Madame Ida Rubinstein, 1928.
— autograph manuscript, piano, 1928. Robert Owen
Lehman Collection, on deposit.

Le Chant du Rossignol (*Song of the Nightingale*).
Commissioned and produced by Diaghilev's Ballets
Russes, 1920.
— autograph manuscript, full score, 1917. Robert
Owen Lehman Collection, on deposit.
— autograph manuscript, sketches, 1916–17. Robert
Owen Lehman Collection, on deposit. p. 29

Firebird (*L'Oiseau de Feu*). Commissioned and
produced by Diaghilev's Ballets Russes, 1910.
— autograph manuscript, piano, extensive revisions
in the composer's hand, [1910], inscribed 1918.
Robert Owen Lehman Collection, on deposit.
pp. 48, 54
— first edition of the score with numerous
annotations and revisions in the composer's
hand. Moscow: P. Jurgenson, [n.d.]. Robert Owen
Lehman Collection, on deposit. p. 55
— autograph manuscript, violin and piano
arrangement of "Prélude et ronde des princesses,"
1926. Mary Flagler Cary Music Collection; Cary 202.
— orchestral score, copyist manuscript, likely
created by Stravinsky's first wife Catherine, [1910].
Extensive conductor's markings and numerous
revisions in the composer's hand. From the library
of Serge Diaghilev. Mary Flagler Cary Music
Collection; Cary 55.
— set of orchestral parts, copyist manuscript,
ca. 1910–29. Annotated by musicians. From
the library of Serge Diaghilev. Mary Flagler Cary
Music Collection; PMC 88–89. p. 18

Fireworks (*Feu d'Artifice*). Produced as a ballet
by Diaghilev's Ballets Russes, 1917.
— print edition with annotations and revisions in
the composer's hand. London: Schott & Co.; Mainz:
B. Schott's Söhne, [1910]. Robert Owen Lehman
Collection, on deposit.

Jeu de Cartes (Card Game). Produced by George
Balanchine with the American Ballet, 1937.
— proof copy with corrections in the composer's
hand. Mainz: B. Schott's Söhne, [ca. 1937]. Mary
Flagler Cary Music Collection; PMC 318.

Les Noces. Commissioned and produced by
Diaghilev's Ballets Russes, 1923.
— autograph manuscript, first draft in short score
(particell) of the first tableau (to rehearsal [16]
in the published score), versions 1–3, [1914–15].
Vellum cover hand-painted by Stravinsky. Robert
Owen Lehman Collection, on deposit. p. 84
— autograph manuscript, two pages of full-score
instrumental sketches for the third tableau,
[1914–15]. Robert Owen Lehman Collection, on
deposit. p. 86
— autograph manuscript drafts for pianola
arrangement, ca. 1919. Mary Flagler Cary Music
Collection, purchased with the special assistance of
the Ann and Gordon Getty Foundation; Cary 567.
p. 87
— proof copy with corrections in the composer's
hand. London: J. & W. Chester, [1922]. Mary Flagler
Cary Music Collection; PMC 319.

Perséphone. Commissioned and produced by
Ida Rubinstein, 1934.
— autograph manuscript, short score (particell),
1934. Mary Flagler Cary Music Collection, gift of
Robert Owen Lehman; Cary 516.

Petrouchka. Commissioned and produced by
Diaghilev's Ballets Russes, 1911.
— autograph manuscript, full score, 26 May 1911.
Robert Owen Lehman Collection, on deposit. p. 57
— full score, revised version, 1946. Robert Owen
Lehman Collection, on deposit.
— *Three Movements from Petrushka*, autograph
manuscript, piano, 1921. Robert Owen Lehman
Collection, on deposit.

Podblyudniye: Four Russian Peasant Songs,
for women's voices, 1917. Composed in part as
preparation for *Les Noces*.
— autograph manuscript. Mary Flagler Cary Music
Collection; Cary 525.

Ragtime. Produced as a ballet by Bronislava
Nijinska's Theatre Choréographique Nijinska
[*sic*], 1925.
— autograph manuscript, piano, 1918. Robert Owen
Lehman Collection, on deposit.

Le Renard. Commissioned and produced by
Diaghilev's Ballets Russes, 1922.
— autograph manuscript, short score (particell)
draft, 1916. Robert Owen Lehman Collection, on
deposit. p. 31

Additional Works

Georges Auric (1899–1983), *La Concurrence*. Produced with choreography by George Balanchine, 1931.
— autograph manuscript, full score, 1931. The Morgan Library Music Collection, purchased as the gift of Howard Phipps Jr., and Henry S. Ziegler.

Georges Auric (1899–1983), *Les Matelots*. Commissioned and produced by Diaghilev's Ballets Russes, 1925.
— autograph manuscript, two pianos, four hands, 1924. Mary Flagler Cary Music Collection, purchased 2022; Cary 726.

Manuel de Falla (1876–1946), "Farruca" from *Le Tricorne*. Commissioned and produced by Diaghilev's Ballets Russes, 1919.
— autograph manuscript, piano, 1918. Dedication to Serge Diaghilev. The Morgan Library Music Collection, gift of Robert Owen Lehman, 1972. p. 27

Reynaldo Hahn (1874–1947), *Le Dieu Bleu*. Commissioned and produced by Diaghilev's Ballets Russes, 1912.
— manuscript in the composer's and copyist's hands, 1912. Mary Flagler Cary Music Collection, purchased 2021; Cary 723.

Arthur Honegger (1892–1955), *Jeanne d'Arc au Bûcher*. Commissioned and produced by Ida Rubinstein, 1938.
— autograph manuscript, vocal/short score, 1935. Dedication to Ida Rubinstein. The Morgan Library Music Collection, gift of Robert Owen Lehman.

Arthur Honegger (1892–1955), *Skating Rink*. Produced by the Ballets Suédois, Rolf de Maré, 1922.
— autograph manuscript, sketches, 1921. With sketches for *Cantique de Pâques* (1918), *La Tempête* (1923), and unidentified music. Robert Owen Lehman Collection, on deposit.

Modest Mussorgsky (1839–1881), *Khovanshchina*. Produced by Diaghilev's Ballets Russes, 1913. Completed and orchestrated by Nikolai Rimsky-Korsakov with passages orchestrated by Maurice Ravel and Igor Stravinsky.
— autograph manuscript excerpt, [1872–81]. James Fuld Collection.

Francis Poulenc (1899–1963), *Les Biches*. Commissioned and produced by Diaghilev's Ballets Russes, 1924.
— copyist's manuscript, vocal score with numerous annotations and revisions in the composer's hand, 1923. Mary Flagler Cary Music Collection, purchased 2020; Cary 721.1.
— autograph manuscript, choral score, 1923. Mary Flagler Cary Music Collection, purchased 2020; Cary 721.2.
— autograph notes for the mise-en-scène, 1931. Mary Flagler Cary Music Collection, purchased 2020; Cary 721.3.

Francis Poulenc (1899–1963), "Discours du Général" from *Les Mariés de la Tour Eiffel*. A ballet by Jean Cocteau commissioned and produced by the Ballets Suédois, 1921, with music by five members of *Les Six*: Georges Auric, Arthur Honegger, Darius Milhaud, Francis Poulenc, and Germaine Tailleferre.
— autograph manuscript, piano, 1921. Mary Flagler Cary Music Collection; Cary 479.

Sergey Prokofiev (1891–1953), *Le Pas d'Acier*. Commissioned and produced by Diaghilev's Ballets Russes, 1927.
— autograph manuscript, piano, ca. 1925. Robert Owen Lehman Collection, on deposit.

Sergey Prokofiev (1891–1953), *Trapèze*. Chamber ballet produced in 1925.
— autograph manuscript, 1925. Robert Owen Lehman Collection, on deposit.

Erik Satie (1866–1925), *Parade*. Commissioned and produced by Diaghilev's Ballets Russes, 1917.
— autograph manuscript, musical quotation, [1917–25]. Mary Flagler Cary Music Collection, purchased 2023; Cary 727.

Piotr Tchaikovsky (1840–1893), *Swan Lake* (*Le Lac des Cygnes*). Produced by Diaghilev's Ballets Russes, 1911 in a condensed two-act version of the original 1895 production at the Maryinsky Theater, St. Petersburg.
— Diaghilev's revised version with annotated printed pages and manuscript pages, 1911. Paris: Mackar & Noël, [1901–7]. From the library of Serge Diaghilev. Mary Flagler Cary Music Collection; PMC 86.

Selected Reading

The following list offers entry to the vast literature on the Ballets Russes, its associated figures, and artistic and cultural trends of the time. After the opening section on Serge Diaghilev's Ballets Russes, it is organized by topic: music, dance, and design; then by the major figures featured in this book.

Diaghilev's Ballets Russes

Auclair, Mathias, and Pierre Vidal. *Les Ballets Russes*. Montreuil: Gorcuff Gradenigo; Paris: Bibliothèque Nationale de France, 2009. Exhibition catalogue.

Baer, Nancy Van Norman, ed. *The Art of Enchantment: Diaghilev's Ballets Russes, 1909–1929*. San Francisco: Fine Arts Museums of San Francisco; New York: Universe Books, 1988. Exhibition catalogue.

Bellow, Juliet. *Modernism on Stage: The Ballets Russes and the Parisian Avant-Garde*. New York: Ashgate, 2013.

Bowlt, John E., and Lynn Garafola, eds. "Sergei Diaghilev and the Ballets Russes: A Tribute to the First Hundred Years." Special issue, *Experiment: Journal of Russian Culture* 17, no. 1 (January 2011).

Caddy, Davinia. *The Ballets Russes and Beyond: Music and Dance in Belle-Époque Paris*. Cambridge: Cambridge University Press, 2012.

Christiansen, Rupert. *Diaghilev's Empire: How the Ballets Russes Enthralled the World*. New York: Farrar, Straus and Giroux, 2022.

Fitzgerald, Clare, ed. *Hymn to Apollo: The Ancient World and the Ballets Russes*. New York: Institute for the Study of the Ancient World, New York University; Princeton: Princeton University Press, 2019. Exhibition catalogue.

Garafola, Lynn. *Diaghilev's Ballets Russes*. New York: Oxford University Press, 1989.

Garafola, Lynn, and Nancy Van Norman Baer, eds. *The Ballets Russes and Its World*. New Haven: Yale University Press, 1999.

García-Márquez, Vicente. *Massine: A Biography*. New York: Alfred A. Knopf, 1995.

Grigoriev, S. L. *The Diaghilev Ballet, 1909–1929*. Edited and translated by Vera Bowen. London: Constable, 1953.

Jeschke, Claudia, and Nicole Haitzinger. *Schwäne und Feuervögel: Die Ballets Russes, 1909–1929. Russische Bildwelten in Bewegung*. [Leipzig]: Henschel, [2009].

Kahane, Martine, and Nicole Wild. *Les Ballets Russes à l'Opéra*. Paris: Hazan/Bibliothèque Nationale de France, 1992.

Kochno, Boris. *Diaghilev and the Ballets Russes*. Translated by Adrienne W. Foulke. New York: Harper & Row, 1970.

Macdonald, Nesta. *Diaghilev Observed by Critics in England and the United States, 1911–1929*. New York: Dance Horizons; London: Dance Books, 1975.

Murga Castro, Idoia. *Pintura en danza: Los artistas españoles y el ballet (1916–1962)*. Madrid: Consejo Superior de Investigaciones Científicas, 2012.

Näslund, Erik, ed. *Ballets Russes: The Stockholm Collection*. Stockholm: Dansmuseet, 2009. Exhibition catalogue.

Pritchard, Jane, ed. *Diaghilev and the Golden Age of the Ballets Russes, 1909–1929*. London: V&A Publishing, 2010. Exhibition catalogue.

Svetlov, Valerian. *Le Ballet contemporain*. Edited in collaboration with Léon Bakst. Translated by M. D. Calvocoressi. St. Petersburg: R. Golicke and A. Willborg, 1912.

Valois, Ninette de. *Invitation to the Ballet*. London: John Lane, The Bodley Head, 1937.

Music

Chimènes, Myriam. *Mécènes et musiciens: Du salon au concert à Paris sous la IIIe République*. Paris: Fayard, 2004.

Davis, Mary E. *Classic Chic: Music, Fashion, and Modernism*. Berkeley: University of California Press, 2006.

Epstein, Louis K. *The Creative Labor of Music: Patronage in Interwar France*. Woodbridge UK: Boydell & Brewer, 2022.

Kahan, Sylvia. *Music's Modern Muse: A Life of Winnaretta Singer, Princesse de Polignac*. Rochester, NY: University of Rochester Press, 2003.

Press, Stephen D. *Prokofiev's Ballets for Diaghilev*. Aldershot, UK: Ashgate, 2006.

Ross, Alex. *Wagnerism: Art and Politics in the Shadow of Music*. New York: Farrar, Straus and Giroux, 2020.

Smart, Mary Ann. *Mimomania: Music and Gesture in Nineteenth-Century Opera*. Berkeley: University of California Press, 2004.

Watkins, Glenn. *Pyramids at the Louvre: Music, Culture, and Collage from Stravinsky to the Postmodernists*. Cambridge, MA: Harvard University Press, 1994.

Dance

Acocella, Joan, and Lynn Garafola, eds. *André Levinson on Dance: Writings from Paris in the Twenties*. Hanover, NH: Wesleyan University Press/University Press of New England, 1991.

Beaumont, Cyril W. *Complete Book of Ballets: A Guide to the Principal Ballets of the Nineteenth and Twentieth Centuries*. London: Putnam, 1937.

Brandenburg, Irene, and Claudia Jeschke. *Tanz Schreiben: Artefakte, Hypertexte—und Nijinsky*. Tanz & Archiv: Forschungsreisen 10. Munich: Epodium, 2023.

Duncan, Isadora. *My Life*. New York: Liveright, 1927.

The Grolier Club of New York. *Four Hundred Years of Dance Notation*. New York: The Grolier Club of New York, 1986.

Homans, Jennifer. *Mr. B: George Balanchine's 20th Century*. New York: Random House, 2022.

Jones, Susan. *Literature, Modernism, and Dance*. Oxford: Oxford University Press, 2013.

Jordan, Stephanie. *Moving Music: Dialogues with Music in Twentieth-Century Ballet*. London: Dance Books, 2000.

Karsavina, Tamara. *Theatre Street: The Reminiscences of Tamara Karsavina*. With a foreword by J. M. Barrie. London: William Heinemann, 1930.

Kirstein, Lincoln. *Movement & Metaphor: Four Centuries of Ballet*. New York: Praeger Publishers, 1970.

Levinson, André. *La Danse d'aujourd'hui: Études, notes, portraits*. Paris: Duchartre et Van Buggenhoudt, 1929.

Levinson, André. *Ballet Old and New*. Translated by Susan Cook Summer. New York: Dance Horizons, 1982.

Pakes, Anna. *Choreography Invisible: The Disappearing Work of Dance*. New York: Oxford University Press, 2020.

Pazcoguin, Georgina. *Swan Dive: The Making of a Rogue Ballerina*. New York: Henry Holt and Company, 2021.

Pouillaude, Frédéric. *Unworking Choreography: The Notion of the Work in Dance*. Oxford: Oxford University Press, 2017.

Pritchard, Jane. *Anna Pavlova: Twentieth Century Ballerina*. With Caroline Hamilton. London: Booth-Clibborn, 2012.

Reynolds, Nancy, and Malcolm McCormick. *No Fixed Points: Dance in the Twentieth Century*. New Haven: Yale University Press, 2021.

Stipanovich, Alexandre. "Meet Kandis Williams and Her Dancing Bodies." *Interview Magazine*, 29 December 2021.

Volynsky, Akim L. *Ballet's Magic Kingdom: Selected Writings on Dance in Russia, 1911–1925*. Translated and edited by Stanley J. Rabinowitz. New Haven: Yale University Press, 2008.

Design

Bell, Robert, and Christine Dixon. *Ballets Russes: The Art of Costume*. Canberra: National Gallery of Australia. Exhibition catalogue.

Bowlt, John E. *The Silver Age: Russian Art of the Early Twentieth Century and the "World of Art" Group*. Newtonville, MA: Oriental Research Partners, 1979.

Bowlt, John E., Zelfira Tregulova, and Nathalie Rosticher Giordano. *A Feast of Wonders: Sergei Diaghilev and the Ballets Russes*. Milan: Skira, 2009. Exhibition catalogue.

Parton, Anthony. *Goncharova: The Art and Design of Natalia Goncharova*. Woodbridge, UK: Antique Collectors' Club, 2010.

Richardson, John. *A Life of Picasso: The Triumphant Years, 1917–1932*. With Marilyn McCully. New York: Alfred A. Knopf, 2007.

Scheijen, Sjeng, ed. *Working for Diaghilev*. Groningen, Netherlands: Groninger Museum, 2004. Exhibition catalogue.

Schouvaloff, Alexander. *The Art of Ballets Russes: The Serge Lifar Collection of Theater Designs, Costumes, and Paintings at the Wadsworth Atheneum, Hartford, Connecticut*. New Haven: Yale University Press and the Wadsworth Atheneum, 1997. Exhibition catalogue.

Léon Bakst

Alexandre, Arsène. *L'Art décoratif de Léon Bakst*. With commentary by Jean Cocteau. Paris: Maurice de Brunhoff, 1913.

Bakst, Léon. *The Designs of Léon Bakst for "The Sleeping Princess": A Ballet in Five Acts after Perrault*. With a preface by André Levinson. London: Benn Brothers, 1923.

Levinson, André. *Bakst: Story of the Artist's Life*. London: Bayard Press, 1923.

Potter, Michelle. "Designed for Dance: The Costumes of Léon Bakst and the Art of Isadora Duncan." *Dance Chronicle* 13, no. 2 (1990): 154–69.

Pruzhan, Irina. *Léon Bakst: Set and Costume Designs, Book Illustrations, Paintings and Graphic Works*. Translated by Arthur Shkarovski-Raffé. New York: Viking, 1987.

Schouvaloff, Alexander. *Léon Bakst: The Theatre Art*. New York: Sotheby Parke Bernet, 1991.

Alexandre Benois

Benois, Alexandre. "Beseda o balete" [Colloquy on ballet]. In V. Meyerhold et al., *Teatr*. St. Petersburg: Shipnovik, 1908: 100–121.

Benois, Alexandre. *Reminiscences of the Russian Ballet*. Translated by Mary Britnieva. London: Putnam, 1941.

Benois, Alexandre. *Alexandre Benois, 1870–1960: Drawings for the Ballet*. With an introduction by Richard Buckle. London: Hazlitt, Gooden & Fox, 1980. Exhibition brochure.

Melani, Pascale. "Inédit: extraits des carnets d'Alexandre Benois, Archives Dimitri Vicheney, Paris." *Slavica Occitania* 23 (2006): 131–57.

Claude Debussy

Antokoletz, Elliott, and Marianne Wheeldon, eds. *Rethinking Debussy*. New York: Oxford University Press, 2011.

Austin, William W., ed. *Debussy: Prelude to "The Afternoon of a Faun."* Norton Critical Scores. New York: W. W. Norton & Company, 1970.

Debussy, Claude. *Correspondance, 1872–1918*. Edited by François Lesure and Denis Herlin. Paris: Gallimard, 2005.

Debussy, Claude. *Debussy Letters*. Edited by François Lesure and Roger Nichols. Translated by Roger Nichols. Cambridge, MA: Harvard University Press, 1987.

Debussy, Claude. *Prélude à l'après-midi d'un faune: Fac-similé du manuscrit autographe de la partition d'orchestre*. Presented by Denis Herlin. Volume 1 of *De main de maître*. Paris: Bibliothèque Nationale de France; Turnhout: Brepols Publishers, 2014.

Dietschy, Marcel. *A Portrait of Claude Debussy*. Edited and translated by William Ashbrook and Margaret G. Cobb. Oxford: Clarendon Press, 1990.

Lesure, François. *Claude Debussy: A Critical Biography*. Edited and translated by Marie Rolf. Rochester, NY: University of Rochester Press, 2019.

Lockspeiser, Edward. *Debussy: His Life and Mind*. 2 vols. Cambridge: Cambridge University Press, 1978.

Médicis, François de, and Steven Huebner, eds. *Debussy's Resonance*. Rochester, NY: University of Rochester Press, 2018.

Nectoux, Jean-Michel. *Harmonie en bleu et or: Debussy, la musique et les arts*. Paris: Fayard, 2005.

Nichols, Roger. *Debussy Remembered*. London: Faber and Faber, 1992.

Orledge, Robert. *Debussy and the Theatre*. Cambridge: Cambridge University Press, 1982.

Rolf, Marie. "Orchestral Manuscripts of Claude Debussy: 1892–1905." *The Musical Quarterly* 70, no. 4 (Autumn 1984): 538–66.

Snyder, Harvey Lee. *"Afternoon of a Faun": How Debussy Created a New Music for the Modern World*. Milwaukee, WI: Amadeus, 2015.

Walsh, Stephen. *Debussy: A Painter in Sound*. New York: Alfred A. Knopf, 2018.

Wenk, Arthur. *Claude Debussy and the Poets*. Berkeley: University of California Press, 1976.

Woodfull-Harris, Douglas, ed. *Debussy: Prélude à l'après-midi d'un faune*. Bärenreiter Urtext Edition. Kassel, Germany: Bärenreiter, 2011.

Serge Diaghilev

Buckle, Richard. *Diaghilev*. New York: Atheneum, 1979.

Buckle, Richard. *In Search of Diaghilev*. New York: Thomas Nelson & Sons, 1956.

Haskell, Arnold L. *Diaghileff: His Artistic and Private Life*. In collaboration with Walter Nouvel. London: Victor Gollancz, 1935.

Lifar, Serge. *Serge Diaghilev: His Life, His Work, His Legend; An Intimate Biography*. New York: G. P. Putnam & Sons, 1940.

Scheijen, Sjeng. *Diaghilev: A Life*. Translated by Jane Hedley-Prôle and S. J. Leinbach. Oxford: Oxford University Press, 2009.

Zil'berstein, I. S., and V. A. Samkov, eds. *Sergei Diagilev i russkoe iskusstvo: stat'i, otkrytye pisma, interv'iu, perepiska*. 2 vols. Moscow: Iskusstvo, 1982.

Michel Fokine

Beaumont, Cyril W. *Michel Fokine and His Ballets*. London: C. W. Beaumont, 1935.

Fokine, Michel. "The New Russian Ballet," letter to the editor. *The Times* (London), 6 July 1914, 6.

Fokine, Michel. *Memoirs of a Ballet Master*. Edited by Anatole Chujoy. Translated by Vitale Fokine. Boston: Little, Brown and Company, 1961.

Horwitz, Dawn Lille. *Michel Fokine*. Boston: Twayne Publishers, 1985.

Kirstein, Lincoln. *Fokine*. With an introduction by Arnold L. Haskell. The Artists of the Dance 12. London: British-Continental Press, 1934.

Bronislava Nijinska

Baer, Nancy Van Norman. *Bronislava Nijinska: A Dancer's Legacy*. San Francisco: Fine Art Museums of San Francisco, 1986. Exhibition catalogue.

Bronislava Nijinska—Svadebka Archives (2019–2023). An electronic book intended to make available, in an interactive form, the Bronislava Nijinska Collection of the Library of Congress concerning *Les Noces* (*Svadebka*). Designed by Dominique Brun, Ivan Chaumeille, and Sophie Jacotot. French translation from Russian by Mariia Nevzorova, texts collected and presented by Ivan Chaumeille. Subsidized by and available at the Centre National de la Danse in Pantin.

Garafola, Lynn. *La Nijinska: Choreographer of the Modern*. New York: Oxford University Press, 2022.

Jeschke, Claudia. "*Les Noces*—Repetition: Variation: Transformation. Bronislawa Nijinska als Choreographin." In *Zur Ästhetik des Vorläufigen*, edited by Thomas Hochradner and Sarah Haslinger, 105–19. Heidelberg: Universitätsverlag Winter, 2014.

Martin, John. "The Dance: Revival of Nijinska's 'Les Noces.'" *New York Times*, 3 May 1936, X7.

Nijinska, Bronislava. "Creation of 'Les Noces.'" Translated with an introduction by Jean M. Serafetinides and Irina Nijinska. *Dance Magazine* (December 1974): 58–61.

Nijinska, Bronislava. *Bronislava Nijinska: Early Memoirs*. Edited and translated by Irina Nijinska and Jean Rawlinson with an introduction by Anna Kisselgoff. Durham: Duke University Press, 1981.

Vaslav Nijinsky

Buckle, Richard. *Nijinsky*. New York: Simon and Schuster, 1971.

Gross, Valentine. *Nijinsky on Stage: Action Drawings by Valentine Gross of Nijinsky and the Diaghilev Ballet Made in Paris between 1909 and 1913*. With an introduction and notes by Richard Buckle. London: Studio Vista, 1971.

Guest, Ann Hutchinson, and Claudia Jeschke. *Nijinsky's "Faune" Restored: A Study of Vaslav Nijinsky's 1915 Dance Score; "L'après-midi d'un faune" and His Dance Notation Method*. Language of Dance Series 3. Binsted, UK: The Noverre Press, 1991.

Guest, Ann Hutchinson, Claudia Jeschke, and Philippe Néagu. *Afternoon of a Faun: Mallarmé, Debussy, Nijinsky*. Edited by Jean-Michel Nectoux. Translated by Maximilian Vos. New York: Vendome Press, 1987. Exhibition catalogue.

Hodson, Millicent. *Nijinsky's Crime against Grace: Reconstruction Score of the Original Choreography for "Le Sacre du Printemps."* Stuyvesant, NY: Pendragon Press, 1996.

Järvinen, Hanna. *Dancing Genius: The Stardom of Vaslav Nijinsky*. New York: Palgrave Macmillan, 2014.

Kirstein, Lincoln. *Nijinsky Dancing*. New York: Alfred A. Knopf, 1975.

Krasovskaya, Vera. *Nijinsky*. Translated by John Bowlt. New York: Schirmer Books, 1979.

Neumeier, John, and Jean-Albert Cartier. *Tanz der Farben: Nijinskys Auge und die Abstraktion*. Hamburg: Hamburger Kunsthalle, 2009. Exhibition catalogue.

Nijinsky, Romola. *Nijinsky*. London: Victor Gollancz, 1933.

Nijinsky, Vaslav. *The Diary of Vaslav Nijinsky: Unexpurgated Edition*. Edited by Joan Acocella. Translated by Kyril FitzLyon. New York: Farrar, Straus and Giroux, 1999; repr. Urbana and Chicago: University of Illinois Press, 2006.

Svobodny, Nicole. *Nijinsky's Feeling Mind: The Dancer Writes, the Writer Dances*. New York: Lexington Books, 2023.

Maurice Ravel

Cahiers Maurice Ravel. Fondation Maurice Ravel. Paris: Éditions Séguier, 1985–ongoing.

Cornejo, Manuel, ed. *L'Intégrale: Correspondance (1895–1936), écrits et entretiens*. Paris: Le Passeur, 2018.

Dru, François, and Quentin Hindley, eds. *Bolero*. Ravel Edition, vol. 1. Linkebeek, Belgium: XXI Music Publishing, 2018.

Dru, François, ed. *La Valse*. Ravel Edition, vol. 8. Linkebeek, Belgium: XXI Music Publishing, 2022.

Goss, Madeleine. *Bolero: The Life of Maurice Ravel*. New York: Tudor Publishing Company, 1945.

Jourdain-Morhange, Hélène, and Vlado Perlemuter. *Ravel According to Ravel*. Edited by Harold Taylor. Translated by Frances Tanner. London: Kahn and Averill, 1988.

Marnat, Marcel. *Maurice Ravel*. Paris: Fayard, 1986.

Mawer, Deborah, ed. *The Cambridge Companion to Ravel*. Cambridge: Cambridge University Press, 2000.

Mawer, Deborah. *The Ballets of Maurice Ravel: Creation and Interpretation*. Aldershot, UK: Ashgate, 2006.

Nichols, Roger. *Ravel*. New Haven: Yale University Press, 2011.

Orenstein, Arbie. *Ravel: Man and Musician*. New York: Columbia University Press, 1975.

Orenstein, Arbie, ed. *A Ravel Reader: Correspondence, Articles, Interviews*. New York: Columbia University Press, 1990.

Roland-Manuel. *Ravel*. Paris: Éditions de la Nouvelle Revue Critique, 1938.

Ida Rubinstein

Chazin-Bennahum, Judith. *Ida Rubinstein: Revolutionary Dancer, Actress, and Impresario.* Albany: State University of New York Press, 2022.

Cossart, Michael de. *Ida Rubinstein: A Theatrical Life.* Liverpool Historical Studies 2. Liverpool: Liverpool University Press, 1987.

Depaulis, Jacques. *Ida Rubinstein: Une inconnue jadis célèbre.* Paris: Éditions Honoré Champion, 1995.

Garafola, Lynn. *Legacies of Twentieth-Century Dance.* Middletown, CT: Wesleyan University Press, 2005.

Lécroart, Pascal, ed. *Ida Rubinstein: Une utopie de la synthèse des arts à l'épreuve de la scène.* Besançon: Presses Universitaires de Franche-Comté, 2008.

Rubinstein, Ida. "Les aspects de la vie moderne: 'L'Art aux trois visages.' Conférence de Mme Ida Rubinstein." *Conferencia: Journal de l'Université des Annales* 19, no. 7 (15 March 1925): 328–42.

Woolf, Vicki. *Dancing in the Vortex: The Story of Ida Rubinstein.* New York: Routledge, 2000.

Igor Stravinsky

Cross, Jonathan, ed. *The Cambridge Companion to Stravinsky.* Cambridge: Cambridge University Press, 2003.

Griffiths, Graham. *Stravinsky's Piano: Genesis of a Musical Language.* New York: Cambridge University Press, 2013.

Jordan, Stephanie. *Stravinsky Dances: Re-Visions across a Century.* Alton, UK: Dance Books, 2007.

Joseph, Charles. "Stravinsky Manuscripts in the Library of Congress and the Pierpont Morgan Library." *The Journal of Musicology* 1, no. 3 (July 1982): 327–37.

Joseph, Charles M. *Stravinsky and the Piano.* Ann Arbor, MI: UMI Research Press, 1983.

Levitz, Tamara. *Modernist Mysteries: Perséphone.* Oxford: Oxford University Press, 2012.

Mazo, Margarita. "Igor Stravinsky's *Les Noces*, the Rite of Passage.'" In *Les Noces (Svadebka).* London: Chester Music, 2005, v–xxi.

Meyer, Felix, ed. *Settling New Scores: Music Manuscripts from the Paul Sacher Foundation.* New York: Schott, 1998.

Neff, Severine, Maureen Carr, and Gretchen Horlacher, eds. *The Rite of Spring at 100.* With a foreword by Stephen Walsh and with John Reef. Bloomington: Indiana University Press, 2017.

Pasler, Jann, ed. *Confronting Stravinsky: Man, Musician, and Modernist.* Berkeley: University of California Press, 1986.

Stravinsky, Igor. *L'Oiseau de feu: Fac-simile du manuscrit Saint-Pétersbourg, 1909–1910.* With studies and commentary by Louis Cyr, Jean-Jacques Eigeldinger, and Pierre Wissmer. Geneva: Conservatoire de Musique de Genève / Minkoff, 1985.

Stravinsky, Vera, and Robert Craft. *Stravinsky in Pictures and Documents.* New York: Simon and Schuster, 1978.

Taruskin, Richard. *Stravinsky and the Russian Traditions: A Biography of the Works through "Mavra."* 2 vols. Berkeley: University of California Press, 1996.

Walsh, Stephen. *Stravinsky: A Creative Spring: Russia and France, 1882–1934.* New York: Alfred A. Knopf, 1999.

Wachtel, Andrew, ed. *Petrushka: Sources and Contexts.* Evanston, IL: Northwestern University Press, 1998.

White, Eric Walter. *Stravinsky: The Composer and His Works.* 2nd ed. Berkeley: University of California Press, 1984.

Index

The Morgan Library & Museum
Staff and Volunteers

Administration
Colin B. Bailey
Katherine Delaney
Sarah Lees
Jessica Ludwig
Lydia Shaw
Kristina W. Stillman

Collection Information Systems
Sandra Carpenter
Robert Decandido
Lenge Hong
Maria Oldal

Communications and Marketing
Noreen Khalid Ahmad
Christina Ludgood
Chie Xu

Development
Mirabelle Cohen
Eileen Curran
Annie Gamez
Molly Hermes
Hannah Lowe
Caroline Mierins
Hadassah Penn
Lauren Stakias
Kirsten Teasdale
Stacy Welkowitz

Drawings and Prints
Esther Levy
Sarah Mallory
John Marciari
Jennifer Tonkovich
Daniel Tsai

Education
Mary Hogan Camp
Esme Hurlburt
Jennifer Kalter
Kat Kiernan
Nicole Leist
Jessica Pastore

Exhibition and Collection Management
Elizabeth Abbarno
Sholto Ainslie
Nicholas Bastis
Alex Félix
Walsh Hansen
Erika Hernandez Lomas
Anne Reilly-Manalo

Facilities
Esperanza Ayala
Monica Barker-Browne
Jean-Luc Bigord
Beverly Bonnick
Ricardo Browne
Glenvet Cassaberry
Josean Colon
Gerard Dengel
Wilson Gonzalez
Melbourne Green
Eric Grimes
Rodney Grimes
Cortez Hackett
Raheem Johnson
Andrew LeeLam
James McCollough
Marina Mugnano
Gilbert Parrilla
Sonny Patrick
Vernon Pulliam
Javier Rivera
Lidia Rodriguez
Jonathan Scales
David Shim
Bromley Synmoie
Pedro Tejada

Janeth Tenempaguay
Noel Thomas
Catherine Torres
Benjamin Ubiera
Francis White
Cory Williams

Financial Services
Nicholas Danisi
Carmen Mui
Faiyad Islam
Thomas Mercurio
Natalie Molloy
Mary Schlitzer

Human Resources
Niekeda Bourgeois
Dorian Lewis-Hood
Eden Solomon

Imaging and Rights
Janny Chiu
Carmen González Fraile
Kaitlyn Krieg
Marilyn Palmeri
Eva Soos
Min Tian

Literary and Historical Manuscripts
Erica Ciallela
Jathan Martin
Philip Palmer
Sarah Robinson

Management Information Systems
Josh Feldman
Dani Frank
Daniel Friedman
Adrian Giannini

Medieval and Renaissance Manuscripts
Deirdre Jackson
Emerald Lucas
Joshua O'Driscoll
Roger Wieck

Merchandising Services
Sherifa Ali-Daniel
Pedro Anlas
Samantha Eberhardt
Aubrey Herr
Alana Hollins
Mahogany Johnson
Michelle Macias
Maya Manaligod
Emily Pritykin
Heloise Robertson
Layla Williams
Stephany Zuleta

Modern and Contemporary Drawings
Emily Roz

Music Manuscripts and Printed Music
Robinson McClellan

Photography
Olivia McCall
Joel Smith

Printed Books and Bindings
Sheelagh Bevan
Jesse Erickson
John McQuillen
Samantha Mohite

Publications
Karen Banks
Yuri Chong
Michael Ferut
Ryan Newbanks

Reading Room
Katherine Graves
Sylvie Merian
María Isabel Molestina
Victoria Stratis

Reference Collection
Peter Gammie
Alaina Poppiti
Sima Prutkovsky

Thaw Conservation Center
Michael Caines
Maria Fredericks
Elizabeth Gralton
Jonathan Johansen
Rebecca Pollak
Yungjin Shin
Reba Fishman Snyder
Francisco Trujillo
Ian Umlauf

Visitor Services
Afra Annan
Aidan Carroll
Simon Cooper
Mae Cote
Laura Fowler
Britney Franco
Tendajie Leon
Leah Marangos
Yvette Mugnano
Elliot Nuss
William Pardoe
Sabrina Rivera
Michelle Volpe

Part-Time Educators
Gema Alava-Crisostomo
William Ambler
Azadeh Amiri Sahameh
Lauren Ball
Dina Gerasia
Nadja Hansen
Rukhshan Haque
Sarah Harris Weiss
Catherine Hernandez
Helen Lee
Mary-Linda Lipsett
Emily Long
Deborah Lutz
Belbelin Mojica
Benjamin Moore
Luned Palmer
Klara Seddon
Walter Srebnick
Maria Yoon

Temporary Art Handlers and Registrars
Fidel Alleyne
Batja Bell
Lauren Clark
James Cullinane
Storm Harper
Junichiro Ishida
Thomas Kotik
Christopher Lesnewski
Meghan Magee
Dustin McBride
Kate McKenzie
Travis Molkenbur
Carolyn Morris
Gary Olson
Yoshinari Oshiro
Beverly Parsons
David Peterson
Anibal Rodriguez
James Sheehan

Volunteers
Sidney Babcock
Grace Brodsky
Mitchell Cohn
Deb Freeman
Judith Hill
Lois Hoffman
Cynthia Johnson
Liz Kaufman
Dede Kessler
Richard Kutner
Sara Lishinsky
Wendy Luftig
Fanette Pollack
Rick Mathews
Cathleen McLoughlin
Joseph Mendez
Carissa Montgomery
Dominique Picon
Pat Pilkonis
Susan Price
Leili Saber
Jacqueline Topche
Jean Vezeris
William Voelkle
Miryam Wasserman
Christie Yang

Current as of 1 January 2024

Curator's Acknowledgments

Conceiving and assembling this exhibition and catalogue often felt like attempting to capture, in fixed form, a body in motion. Like a dancer whose movements can never be experienced fully except in live performance, the hundreds of objects I considered seemed to rebel at being pinned down into a single, static list. For each design, manuscript, and first-person account there were always many others contending for inclusion, each capturing the same ballet in its many aspects, each opening different glimpses into its conception and creation.

In this impossible endeavor I have been lucky in those who have advised and supported me. I would like to extend my thanks above all to Robin Lehman, whose taste and passion made his collection the magnificent musical gathering it is, not only in the domain of ballet but far beyond, and for his support and key suggestions; to Marie Rolf, whose deep understanding of this domain and wise counsel ensured this project's excellence; to Lynn Garafola, whose profound knowledge of Diaghilev's Ballets Russes and its universe is unequalled, and whose generous advice at every level of the exhibition and catalogue went well beyond her own essay in this volume; and to Claudia Jeschke, whose pioneering work and subtle discernment in the art of dance notation has been a revelation to me and allowed this exhibition to broach new territory. I would like to thank the Morgan's Director Colin B. Bailey for his steadfast support for this exhibition and catalogue, his close reading of the material, and his invaluable advice throughout. I am grateful to John Marciari, Charles W. Engelhard Curator of Drawings and Prints, whose steady advisement and enthusiasm kept the project on course and to the highest standard; to Ryan Newbanks and Yuri Chong for their keen editorial presence through the many stages of this book; and to the Fellows from the CUNY Graduate Center, Alexis Rodda, Madison Schindele, and Paola Rodriguez, music scholars who each contributed extensive research, insight from their own realms of expertise, and long conversations with me brainstorming and philosophizing.

A project like this cannot succeed without the support of a broad community of scholarship. I am thankful for my illuminating conversations and correspondence with dance scholars Stephanie Jordan and Jane Pritchard; music scholars Arbie Orenstein, Stephen Roe, Manuel Cornejo, Maureen Carr, Phillip Torbert, Daniel Elphick, Sylvia Kahan, and François Dru for his energy, vital connecting of people, and provision of key sources; curators Libby Smigel and Melissa Wertheimer at the Library of Congress whose warm welcome made possible my revelatory visit to the Bronislava Nijinska and Ida Rubinstein Collections, and Patrick Shepler, who made all things possible with the loaned objects; Linda Murray at the New York Public Library Dance Collection, whose advice yielded key sources; Edward Kasinec, former chief of the Slavonic and Baltic Division at the New York Public Library, who generously offered his deep experience; and for the support of Jennifer Homans and Andrea Salvatore at the Center for Ballet and the Arts, Scott Blackshire at the McNay Art Museum, Matthew Wittmann and Dale Stinchcomb at the Harvard Theatre Collection, Oliver Tostmann and Matthew Hargraves at the Wadsworth Atheneum, Donald Flanell Friedman and Judith Chazin-Bennahum for their insight on the life of Ida Rubinstein, Robert Johnson, and Iain Webb. Special thanks to the Fokine family, Michael, Ursula, Isabelle, and Nicholas, whose discussions exploring the Michel Fokine Archive were especially meaningful; to Dominique Brun, Ivan Chaumeille, Sophie Jacotot, and Mariia Nevzorova, whose translations of Bronislava Nijinska's dance notations opened a crucial window into her creative thinking, and Laurent Barré at the Centre National de la Danse in Pantin for early access to that wonderful resource, and to Sima Prutkovsky at the Morgan for her help with translations. I am indebted to the collectors whose generosity allowed key works to be present, and to David Lowenherz, Gabriel Boyers, and John and Jude Lubrano for key acquisitions related to the exhibition.

An exhibition is a deeply collective phenomenon. I am grateful to all those at the Morgan Library & Museum who have contributed, who number in the hundreds—the engineering team that tends our building, the security staff who ensures the safety of guests and artwork, the visitor services associates who welcome the public, and colleagues in every other department of the Morgan playing vital roles, who are listed in this volume.

A special thanks to my Morgan colleagues whose friendship has been so important through these past fifteen years, Fran Barulich, Linden Chubin, Maria Oldal, María Molestina, Marilyn Palmeri, and Peter Gammie, and to my friends whose advice and repeated close readings made this project possible, Linda Kramer, Nathaniel Leeds, and Tarik O'Regan.

Finally, I am grateful to Stephen Saitas for his vibrant design of the exhibition, and Barbara Glauber of Heavy Meta for her elegant catalogue design.

Robinson McClellan